The Billion Dollar Secret

Secrets to Winning Business from a Former Government Executive

Copyright © 2020 Gloria Parker

ISBN: 9798668810529

Publisher: CornerStone IT, LLC
Author: Gloria Parker
Co-Author: Mike Rice

D1521376

Parker Group Consulting

www.parkergroupconsulting.com

Rev 1.0

Table of Contents

Preface

Authors Gloria Parker and Mike Rice have been working together for almost a decade, in pursuit of both large and small opportunities. Mike was working for a small business when he was introduced to Gloria, who was consulting to that same firm. Gloria worked alongside the Business Development (BD) team, grooming the team's insight into how to successfully engage the Federal Government in pursuit of acquisitions within the firm's pipeline. On one occasion, the BD team received an abbreviated version of Gloria's extensive courseware on effectively managing federal customer engagements.

Gloria was a Chief Information Officer (CIO) at two cabinet agencies of the federal government for ten years. The IBM Corporation employed Gloria for 17 years. IBM recognized Gloria for her exceptional ability to apply technology to meet the business needs of her customers. She held high-level management and executive positions and received many awards, including the prestigious "IBM Golden Circle" recognition for exemplary leadership; presented to the top 1% of personnel. Gloria's insight into successfully penetrating the federal marketplace comes from the unique opportunity of sitting on both sides of the table. Gloria's advice, based on that "two-chair" view, has been coveted across the public and private executive landscape.

In 2018, Mike left the firm and focused on developing the "In Pursuit - Business Development Life Cycle."[1] The Life Cycle's framework lifts the best from Large Business BD methodologies and tailors them for Small and Mid-Tier firms to ensure a sustainable, revenue-healthy pipeline into the federal marketplace. Upon completion of the Life Cycle, Mike reached out to Gloria about developing a small topical companion book for the series based on the abbreviated training he received from Gloria just a few years previous. Gloria's response was simple, "Mike, you only have one small portion of what I teach. Let's talk about the bigger picture. Oh, by the way, I bought your book!"

Gloria's "two-chair" view into doing business with the federal government comprises that Big Picture. Her workshops dive deep into the branches of the U.S. Government, the anatomy of each department, budgeting processes, spending priorities, whom you need to know and why, relationship building, managing your customer engagement, how to develop an opportunity, then compete. The Big Picture expands well outside the Life Cycle's focus.

Today, Gloria provides training to both large and small business executives and business development professionals. One large business committed to training up to 1000 individuals from business

---

[1] *Rice, Mike. In Pursuit – Business Development Life Cycle. CornerStone IT, LLC. ©2019*

development and operations staff with Gloria's courses. In addition to the private sector, Gloria has been contracted to provide management workshops to government top department officials. She actively mentors up and coming government CXO's and has guided many into successful and rewarding government careers. Her wisdom impacts all aspects of business in the Washington DC scene.

The decision was not to write a topical companion to the "In Pursuit" series, but instead, explore capturing Gloria's extensive experience as a top industry and government executive; marketing to and being the focus of a marketing campaign, in written form. Thus, this book. Our hope is that the reader gains a new appreciation of the innerworkings of the federal government's acquisition process.

Introduction

Most business development professionals started their careers doing something other than sales and marketing. They find themselves thrust into the BD (business development) world due to the need of firms to capture new business and to sustain growth. Gloria started with IBM as a system engineer. Mike also started in the IT field as an engineer.

Companies today are beginning to understand the value of their operations team in establishing future business. Note that we said "future" business, not necessarily "new" business. Operations is not the focus of this book. That is a discussion for another time.

Marketing/selling to the Federal Government or any enterprise has often been treated as a quick "hit or miss" event. Business developers/salespeople who think this way have little success. They often wonder why their job is so "difficult"! Successful business developers understand that there is A SYSTEM to selling! Those that understand and utilize the <u>systematic approach</u> almost always win. What is the Systematic Approach?

The system for selling can be summarized in eight (8) phases:
1) Understand the business environment – you have to understand the customer's business in order to understand his/her pain and

what drives them

2) Understand procurement rules – you must make sure you know how to follow the rules of engagement so that you can win and stay out of trouble

3) Understand who's who and who you need to know and subsequently meet with – it is extremely important to call on the right people for the information you need and to know who will make the decisions and who will influence decisions. Also, you will want to know who can help you in the account.

4) Know how to build the relationships you need with the people you need to know

5) Know how to create the mindset of a trusted partner for the customer – a potential customer only wants to work with the company and representative that they feel has their best interest at heart and who is truly knowledgeable about their needs and truly want to help solve the problem, not just sell a widget.

6) Do your research – you have to be seen as an expert before a customer will trust you

7) Know how to get a meeting with the customer

8) Become an expert at conducting a successful customer meeting in which the customer comes out a winner and you also win!

Business Developers understand and operate at these phases at varying levels or degrees of knowledge. It becomes easy to spot those who know how to systematically sell versus those who go about it haphazardly. This results in 4 types of business developers.

Types of Business Development Professionals

The industry is full of Business Development activity. As stated previously, many business development professionals have never been formally taught how to effectively engage in practice. Experience has taught that doing nothing produces nothing, doing some produces little, doing a lot produces some and doing it right produces most. Based on that experience, we've identified four types of practitioners.

Type 1 – Show Up at Events (Doing Nothing)

There is an unfortunate trend within our industry where we see BD professionals move from company to company, usually in 18-month tours, never closing any business. You see them at all the events; attending breakfasts, lunches, dinners, and happy hours. They have mastered the "BD Dance," bragging about who they know, who they just talked to, and handing out their new business card. They tend to know what's going on across the landscape due to asking and listening to other BDer's conversations. Their only exposure to government decision-makers and stakeholders is the result of attending an event where government leadership is either speaking or participating on a topical panel.

These individuals never seem to move into the other practices of business development, coaching the capture manager into how to translate customer need into a winning proposal, because they have no idea of the problem which needs a solution.

After 18 months, these "do-nothings" move on to another firm, get new business cards, and the cycle continues. Hopefully, they are reading this book and have the desire to better their own professional business development skillset.

Type 2 - Find out new opportunities (Doing Some)

Like our Type 1 Pro, this individual attends as many events as possible. Yes, they, too, participate in the BD Dance, however, they have a little more information to share and discuss.

Our Type 2 professionals learn that there are tools available to monitor the acquisition landscape and begin to target potential pursuits for their firm. Most of the information they need is available online through sources like GovWin[2], Bloomberg[3],

---

[2] *https://iq.govwin.com/*
[3] *https://about.bgov.com*

GovTribe4, FedBizOps5, Ebuy 6, USASpending7, FPDS8, or other agency-centric sites. These sites provide all the detail needed to appropriately monitor acquisition activity concerning the opportunity to include the incumbent, along with historical and anticipated solicitation timing.

These individuals lack face-to-face interaction with the government customer. They rely solely on web site data, maybe looking for hints in unexpected period-of-performance or anticipated spend vs. actual spend to guess at the incumbent's strengths or weaknesses. They have never built a relationship with the customer nor a real understanding of the needs of the agency.

I remember a former government CIO, who is now in the industry, tell me that their business development team would populate the pipeline with new information just before the quarterly pipeline review. This information came directly from the sites mentioned above, with no intimate/unique data. This person was a seasoned leader and shrewd leader, and fired the entire BD team. You cannot rely solely on "intel websites" to manage pipeline data. Demand

---

[4] *https://govtribe.com*
[5] *https://www.fbo.gov*
[6] *https://www.ebuy.gsa.gov/*
[7] *https://www.usaspending.gov/*
[8] *https://www.fpds.gov/fpdsng_cms/index.php/en/*

face-to-face information about the agency's needs and acquisition plans.

Type 3 – Understand (Doing A lot)

This individual is high energy, positive, engages in business development events, and has been building relationships with decision-makers in the federal backdrop. Their relationship-building extends into the competitive landscape, as they regularly engage potential partners for future business. The Type 3 professional identifies opportunities early, grooms their pipeline on a consistent rhythm, and qualifies prospective pursuits. They understand their firm's long-term strategy, are aware of the market, and posture their company to represent well in the market.

Type 3 business developers are actively chasing the market but lack the acumen to close the business. They are good on their feet during customer engagements but have never learned the successful formula for closing out the meeting. Although this individual knows how to represent their company's service area offering for customers that they are intimate with, they struggle to engage stakeholders that they do not personally know. In short, they lack the knowledge necessary to close the business with new customers.

Type 4 – Consistent Success (Doing it Right)

The Type 4 individual is our target prototype for the business development professional who is consistently positioning their firm for success. This individual understands the structure of government, who the decision-makers are, federal processes, influences on budget priorities. Our successful professional researches the department or agency and gains a deep understanding of the mission. This professional is aware of lines of business and how changes in priorities and policies impact the lines. When engaging, they have a mindset to connect with the customer, focus on the need of the agency, and establish a relationship of trust with their potential customer. They build rapport, create interest, qualify the customer's expectations, understand the decision-maker needs, present a solution that is need-centric, and handle objections in open dialogue to refine the solution. As the opportunity moves into a proposal process, the business development professional engages with the capture team to properly translate the customer's need and expected solution to ensure a successful win for both the customer and the company.

The Billion Dollar Secret focuses on preparing business development professionals to experience successful pursuits and professional victories. Become a Type 4 Business Developer, immensely valued by the customer and your company.

Challenges Faced by Businesses trying to Market to the Federal Government

The federal marketplace is one of the most challenging markets to penetrate for businesses that try to do business in this environment. It is a vast and very complex organization to navigate. Many rules, regulations, and policies impact your ability to move products and services. The agencies where you are attempting to market your solutions receive direction and priorities from multiple sources. Procurement rules and regulations are very complex and carry severe penalties for breaking the rules even if you didn't know the directive existed.   Relationship building in this environment can take a very long time. Many business developers don't know how to go about building those relationships. Procurement rules are stiff and prevent the typical close social activities that make it easier to develop similar associations in the commercial environment.   In government, although you may have the best solution, you can lose the bid and not understand why!

In this chapter, we will provide you with an overview of the federal structure. We will explain who the players are, the influence that they have. We will also discuss how some of the government structures you usually have not paid much attention to can have a significant impact, both positive and negative, on your marketing goals. One of the most important things you will need to know as a successful business developer is how the government sets priorities and justifies its spending. We will cover that in this chapter as well.

No matter whether you are selling to a commercial company or the federal, state, and local governments, one critical requirement is that you know the business of the organization you are marketing to and that you know their structure and decision-making processes. Let's begin with the Federal Government Structure and Processes.

FEDERAL GOVERNMENT STRUCTURE AND PROCESSES

There are three branches of the Federal Government, and each one plays a role in setting the priorities of the government's purchasing decisions.

Legislative Branch

The legislative branch of the federal government consists of Congress, which has two houses: Senate and House

- **Legislative Branch**
  - Appropriates Agency Budgets
  - Makes Laws That Affect Agency Spending
  - Gets Involved in Decision Making on Contracts When Necessary
- **Judiciary Branch**
  - Interprets Laws That Can Impact Sales

- **Executive Branch**
  - Office of Management and Budget (OMB)
  - Departments (24 CFO Legislated Departments)
  - Administrative Offices (OPM, GSA, SBA)
  - Agencies
  - Investigator General

of Delegates (Congress).

This branch makes the laws of the land. THIS BRANCH REPRESENTS THE PEOPLE OF THE UNITED STATES. We, the people, vote these representatives into office to make laws on our behalf and ensure that the federal government meets the people's needs. They develop and pass legislation that governs how the United States will operate. It is essential to understand that the Legislative branch appropriates funding to the Executive Branch of government to carry out each agency's mission.

The agencies (Executive Branch) will develop a proposed budget based upon the White House's priorities. Once the budget is vetted between the agencies and the White House, it is forwarded to Congress. The appropriations committees of Congress negotiate the budget with the White House. Congress will then make the budget into a bill passed by Congress (both the House and the Senate) to enact the spending plan (budget) into law. Congress has a vested interest in the budget because their job is to ensure that the law protects their constituents (the people they represent in their jurisdictions). Voters get the services of government that they need, and such things as employment, healthcare, infrastructure, and other such services meet the requirement of the legislator's constituents. The organization called the Government Accountability Office (GAO) is the investigative arm of the Congress, and they review the actions of the agencies and recommend fixes to problems of waste, fraud, abuse, budget problems, and other matters. The GAO reports back to Congress on the underperformance or spending violations of the agencies. So, let's put this theory into perspective with a real example. During an acquisition, the unsuccessful awardee may choose to file the protest with the GAO. The GAO will review the procurement decision and will make a recommendation on protest mitigation. I know of a situation where two companies were battling over a substantial procurement, and a Senator had the GAO conduct a review. The Senator managed to hold back funds from the agency to get the agency to change the decision. The Senator was concerned that jobs would be taken from the people in his/her jurisdiction because the other company would move employment to a new state. A very heated battle went on for a long time. Even though the Senator did not get all that was wanted, he/she subtly forced the agency to split the contract between the two vendors. Lesson learned here is to know what all of the stakeholders want and make sure you take all of their needs into consideration when going after an opportunity.

Judiciary Branch

One branch of government that is ignored by most business developers is the Judiciary branch. The Judiciary, led by the Supreme Court, upholds the Constitution. The court brings disagreements of the people of the United States to closure, and their judgment is final. Many cases make their way to the Supreme Court, and the Justices will determine whether they should hear the case elevated to them or not.

There are many examples of recent cases heard by our Supreme Court Justices. Prominent today are cases focused on healthcare, discrimination, immigration, religious freedom, marriage, and corruption.

Most companies never pay attention to the docket of the Supreme Court. Imagine if you were a healthcare company marketing a solution for the Affordable Care Act. If a Supreme Court decision suddenly impacts an opportunity you were pursuing for several years, you wasted a ton of time and money on something that did not stand a chance. A very successful business developer will take the time to follow the Supreme Court's docket to make sure they are not in danger of pursuing an opportunity that may never emerge.

Executive Branch

Most business developers spend 95% or more of their time working with Executive Branch agencies comprised of White House, Cabinet Agencies, Administration Agencies, and other smaller Agencies and Bureaus. This branch of government is in place to carry out the mission of the federal government. At the top of the structure is the White House / President of the United States. Thus, the President's job is to accomplish this mission through the executive departments and agencies. The administrative arm of the White House is known as the Office of Management and Budget (OMB). Housed across the street from the White House, OMB manages finance policies, procurement policies, technology policies. OMB negotiates the budgets for the federal agencies under the President's direction.

Directly reporting to the President are the Cabinet Secretaries and Administrators who are the federal agencies' appointed leadership. Commonly known as CFO (Chief Financial Officer) agencies are 24 large Departments and Agencies. They received that name through the CFO ACT, putting CFO's in each large agency.

They are:

- Department of Agriculture
- Department of Defense
- Department of Energy

- Department of Homeland Security
- Department of Interior
- Department of Labor
- Department of Transportation
- Department of Veterans Affairs
- National Aeronautics and Space Administration
- Federal Emergency Management Agency
- National Science Foundation
- Office of Personnel Management

- Department of Commerce
- Department of Education
- Department of Health and Human Services
- Department of Housing and Urban Development
- Department of Justice
- Department of State
- Department of Treasury
- Environmental Protection Agency

- Agency for International Development
- General Services Administration
- Nuclear Regulatory Commission
- Small Business Administration

The above are the Cabinet Agencies headed by a Cabinet Secretary or Administrator. Typically, when the name ends with "Administration," they are led by an Administrator and represent the White House's administrative arms. If the name starts with "Department," they are headed by Cabinet Secretaries and make up the Cabinet of the President's Office. These are the highest-ranking personnel of the agencies. When your company calls on them, they do not want to hear about speeds, feeds, bits, and bytes. Nor do they want to know the details of your offering. Their focus is on mission and policy and they engage only with industry leadership, typically the President or CEO of the company.

Reporting to the Cabinet Secretaries or Administrators are Deputy Secretaries or Deputy Administrators. These are the individuals who provide backup for the Cabinet Secretaries and Administrators and run the agency's operations. You can view the Cabinet Secretaries as primarily "out-facing" and the Deputy Secretaries as primarily "in-facing."

A Deputy Secretary also only wants to meet with very high-level executives in your company, and their conversation tends to be around policy and mission. In terms of operations, they may want to talk to very successful companies about approaches to managing real estate, restructuring organizations, and responding to COVID-19. However, like their uplines, they do not want to hear about tools, service offerings, and products.

Reporting to the Deputy Secretaries and the Cabinet Secretaries are the Assistant Secretaries and Chiefs. By Chiefs, I mean the CXO's where the X stands for which office Chief they are. They include Chief Financial Officer, Chief Information Officer, Chief Acquisition Officer. Chief Human Capital Officer, Chief

Data Officer, Chief Privacy Officer, and the like. The Assistant Secretaries run particular segments of the department's mission, and the Chiefs run specific operations areas of the agency. For example, at the Department of Housing and Urban Development, you will see Assistant Secretaries running Housing, Public and Indian Housing, Community Planning and Development, Fair Housing, Policy and Research, and others. These individuals want to talk to people about their particular mission challenges and what they can do to move their mission in the specific segment in which they are responsible. Again, they are too high level to talk about speeds and feeds. The Secretary, Assistant Secretaries, and the Deputy Secretary are political appointees in most cases, which means they are appointed by the president and serve at the pleasure of the president instead of being career employees.

Reporting to the Assistant Secretaries and Chiefs are Directors who manage a narrower segment of the mission represented by their assistant secretary. Directors are usually the first level of federal career employees. For example, under Housing, there will be a Director of Multi-Family Housing and a Director of Single-Family Housing. These directors will be interested in talking about solutions to address their mission concerns, but they do not get deep into the details of the product or service. They are laser-focused on how their problem can be solved.

Reporting to the Directors are Branch Chiefs who are the persons that manage a very narrow part of the mission but at a very detailed level. They are the ones who will talk about and know about the details of the opportunity that you are pursuing.

Note that the higher in the organization the person is you are meeting with, the more control they have over the agency's priorities and the budget associated with the opportunity. Consider your audience carefully! You may go down a long road talking to a Branch Chief about a future acquisition you are interested in to find out that suddenly the dollars have been snatched to put on another project. This is not an indication that you are wasting time talking to the Branch Chief. Just the opposite. Branch Chiefs can share details of the opportunity that you cannot get anywhere else, giving you knowledge necessary to formulate a tight solution. It is equally important to get to know the higher-level executives to gain a better understanding of the priorities from the top and how the agency is allocating budget. Understanding the agency's structure, the chain of authority, and budget priorities, you will focus on programs that you are interested in with less risk of having the rug pulled out from under you!

Procurement

have known business development professionals who lack basic
nowledge of the acquisition process within the federal government. The
ocess can be extremely complicated overall; but distilled down to its five
imary phases; you will understand the method.

AR Part 1.102(a) states, *"The vision for the Federal Acquisition System is
deliver on a timely basis the best value product or service to the customer,
hile maintaining the public's trust and fulfilling public policy objectives.
irticipants in the acquisition process should work together as a team and
ould be empowered to make decisions within their area of responsibility."*
ote the emphasis on teamwork. This five-phase lifecycle lends itself to
st that objective, and we are experiencing more integrated project teams
PT's) throughout the acquisition process. Each member brings their
xpertise to the procurement. Creative solicitations leveraging orals,
chnical challenges, and product demos are becoming more common
an written technical volumes. Innovative evaluation techniques such as
nfidence ratings, on the spot consensus, comparative evaluations, and
lvisory down-selects are streamlining procurements across the federal
ndscape—all these procurement innovations fitting within these well-

defined five phases. For more information on Acquisition Innovation visit the Federal Acquisition Institute's Periodic Table[9].

Contract Planning

Contract Planning
- Requirements
- Funding
- Market Research
- Planning
- Contract Type
- Approval

In this phase of the procurement cycle, tl customer and contract officer are determinir how the contract is structured. They a defining the requirements, setting budg priorities, determining vendor communi participation, planning the solicitation ar contract type, and gaining approval to move forward with tl acquisition.

Establishing requirements is the first step in the procurement proces This exercise begins when the Program Office defines the busine need and the approach to satisfy the use case. Securing funding is tl process of looking at budget priorities to ensure that this project hɛ funds for execution. The Program Office (PO) begins its Mark Research, whereby it performs due diligence to ensure that th requirement can or cannot be satisfied with current solutions. Tl PO determines if the product or service already exists, and wheth there is a path to acquire them with a new acquisition. Also, a Sourc Sought, or Request for Information (RFI) may be used to determir

---

[9] *https://www.fai.gov/periodic-table/*

if the Program Office is still developing requirements and is considering products and services that may better satisfy the business need. If the production or service does not exist, the Program Office and Contract Office (CO) begin Acquisition Planning, preparing the strategic approach to meet the government's needs by the most economical and efficient means. This activity is the genesis of the Acquisition Strategy. The strategy defines components of the Solicitation, such as the Contract Type to best satisfy the requirement. Contract Type may be Time and Material (T&M), Labor Hour, Firm Fixed Price (FFP), Cost Plus, or some combination across the Solicitation. Completion of the Acquisition Strategy, Acquisition Plan, and Source Selection Plan indicates that the Solicitation is ready for approval to move into the Solicitation Phase.

Solicitation

The Solicitation phase typically begins with some public announcement that the procurement is about to commence. Pay attention to government procurement sites to ensure that you do not miss the solicitation release. It is common practice for the Program

and Contract Office to engage potential industry partners through the release of draft requirements with the intent to seek comments. Industry Days and Due Diligence meetings with the government are

common to share information and exchange comments. Once th
government is satisfied that they have all they need from the industry
they prepare solicitation documents for release. Dates are determine
for critical milestones, such as vendor Q&A and proposal submissior
within the procurement schedule. Once the solicitation is issued an
all items from interested parties have been satisfied either throug
answers back from the customer or modifications to the solicitatior
the source selection team prepares for receipt of proposal submission:

Evaluation

At this point, all companies have submitte
their proposals, Source Selection begins t
evaluate volumes. The evaluation process
generally standard across agencies with th
Program Office evaluating the technic
volumes and Contract Office assessing pric
If the evaluation board has questions with your technical
management approach, they may ask for clarification on a topic. Th
Contract Office may also ask for your Best and Final Offer (BAFC
to get the best possible price for the government. Both Clarificatic
Questions and BAFO are positive indicators that your proposal is
contender for the award. Source Selection then compiles all scor
and, based on the evaluation criteria stated in the solicitation, sele
the successful awardee.

Award

Typically, the CO notifies the successful awardee first. It's a good idea to keep that information to yourself and not leak the award as a successful firm. Fight the urge to announce and give the government time to notify the unsuccessful awardee(s). In some

cases, the CO instructs you not to announce anything until a certain time. Discretion minimizes negative energy between the government and industry. The Contracting Officer must prepare for debrief requests and potential protests. Debrief typically happens first, and the FAR requires the government to provide a debrief. The FAR also provides tremendous latitude to the government on how to conduct debriefs, whether orally, over the phone or in written form. Protests typically follow the debrief period; however, some protests are filed immediately upon notification of an unsuccessful result. Debriefs and Protests are a discussion for another time. Once the protest period has passed, funds are obligated, and performance commences.

Post Award

As we just discussed, the first 100 days after award may include protest activity. Protests are filed either with the soliciting agency, the Government Accountability Office (GAO) or the U.S. Court of Federal Claims (COFC). In some cases, firms have protested to all three authorities. Remember our discussion on the anatomy of the Federal Government? GAO reports to Congress (Legislative). Court of Federal Claims falls under the Judiciary. The solicitating agency or DoD report directly to the White House (Executive). This engagement of all three branches of government is why it is essential to build and understand your stakeholder map.

Post Award represents the execution of the contract itself. This phase of the acquisition lifecycle carries on throughout the period of performance. Activities such as placing orders against the contract and monitoring contractor performance all fall in the Contract Office's purview. If required, the Program Office and Contract Office will score the vendor's performance through the Contractor Performance Assessment Reporting System (CPARS). Ultimately this phase of the lifecycle ends at the contract closeout.

The Federal Acquisition Regulation (FAR)

Most procurements are subject to what is known as the Federal Acquisition Regulations or the FAR. The FAR is NOT law; it is regulation. Laws govern everyone equally while a regulation only applies to its intended audience; in this case, U.S Federal Government acquisition activity. According to FAR Subpart 1.101 Purpose10, *"The Federal Acquisition Regulations System is established for the codification and publication of uniform policies and procedures for acquisition by all executive agencies. The Federal Acquisition Regulations System consists of the Federal Acquisition Regulation (FAR), which is the primary document, and agency acquisition regulations that implement or supplement the FAR."* The FAR establishes the foundation for acquisition policy across the federal landscape. FAR Subpart 1.301 encourages the development of agency-specific regulations *"that implement or supplement the FAR and incorporate, together with the FAR, agency policies and procedures, contract clauses, solicitation provisions, and forms that govern the contracting process ..."* Please find links to agency-specific procurement regulations, commonly known as agency supplements, on ACQUISITION.gov[11]. These agency supplements

---

[10] *https://acquisition.gov/content/part-1-federal-acquisition-regulations-ystem#id1617MD00E92*

[11] *https://www.acquisition.gov/content/supplemental-regulations*

are generally structured the same as the FAR and further focuses i authority on the issuing agency.

When a procurement is released it follows one of several potenti FAR parts:

- FAR Part 8, Subpart 8.4 Federal Supply Schedules – The Gener Services Administration (GSA) Multiple Award Schedul (MAS)
- FAR Part 12, Acquisition of Commercial Items – policies ar procedures unique to the acquisition of commercial items.
- FAR Part 13, Simplified Acquisition – policies and procedures f the acquisition of supplies and services which do not exceed th simplified acquisition threshold
- FAR Part 15, Contracting by Negotiation – policies ar procedures governing competitive and noncompetitive (so source) negotiated acquisitions.
- FAR § 16.505(b), Fair Opportunity – policies and procedures ar guides selecting a contract type appropriate to the circumstanc of the acquisition.

In researching for this book and my course, I interviewed a procuremer official who provided the following quick quotes:

For Procurement Pros:

- "Procurement Lifecycle is 1st quarter to 3rd quarter"

- "Don't come with new opportunity in 4th quarter"
- "Don't come unprepared"
- "Cross check your data"
- "Don't just drop off collateral"

For Contractors

- "Get on calendar with capabilities that are relevant to the customer's interests"
- "Look at President's budget to understand what the agency will be spending money for"
- "Look at pass back which is the negotiation document between the agency and OMB"
- "In evaluating your proposal, the Government will look for, compliance first, watch your misspellings and grammar and make sure you answered all the questions that were asked."

General

- "FAR is a guidance document; not law"
- "Once an idea is put to paper with $$'s attached, you cannot talk to them. If the government talks to you after this point, you cannot bid"
- "Only procurement personnel can get bids and quotes; anyone can get a ROM (Rough Order of Magnitude)"

- "Unsolicited Proposal – look at supplement to the FAR for t▮ particular agency – it tells you how THAT agency will acce▮ an unsolicited proposal"

Procurement Do's and Don'ts

- "Don't offer tickets and dinners"
- "Do not try to call or talk to agency about procurement aft▮ proposals are submitted unless instructed to do so by t▮ contracting officer"

Who You Need to Know

'e covered the structure of the federal government and who the players e. We also discussed what those players want to talk about and who they ant to talk to. How do you determine who to get to know in the agency here you want to do business? There are several things to consider.

ı initial meetings that you have with people you know, including people ithin the agency or other vendors, find out who will make the decision ı the solution you are interested in selling. Just ask!! Determine if the erson you are pursuing and spending time with is really the person who ın make the decision or at least has knowledge about the opportunity or an influencer. If they are not, you are probably wasting valuable time.

ю your homework to find out who the influencers and decision-makers ·e. You can read articles, listen to customer speeches at events, ask others, .tend industry days at the agency, read all of the information you can get ıout the opportunity, go to the research firm sites where they often state ·ho is in charge of the procurement, and other ways that are discussed .ter in the section on "doing your research". You will want to get to know ıe procurement shop because they are the ones who determine how the ılution will be procured. They decide the procurement vehicles that will e used and many times they determine if the procurement will be based ı value or LPTA (Low Price Technically Acceptable). I have often seen

situations where the business developer has a good enough relationsh
with the procurement team to get the vehicle they want. If you can expla
to the procurement official that a particular direction is in their be
interest, they may listen.

You should definitely spend time in the program or mission area becau
they are the ones with the critical need, and they have the mone
Oftentimes, lower level business developers will not want to call on th
mission people because they feel that the technology folks are the on
that they have to convince. But keep in mind that the technology offi
is in place to support the mission. So, the mission people are custome
of the technology office. It is very important to get to know the missic
people who have the biggest influence in a procurement. And clearly yc
need to get to know the CXO's because they handle the budge
technology, human resource and other support organizations that will l
involved in the decision being made for the right solution.

There is also an exercise that you should complete for every larg
opportunity and sometimes a critical small opportunity that will cause yc
to think through the process of figuring out who you need to know. An
even if you don't know them personally, at least understand who th
stakeholders are so that you can keep up with their position on you
pursuit and know what makes your pursuit important to them. Th
methodology is called a stakeholder mapping. It is a work process b
which you determine who in Congress as well as state and loc

vernments cares about the opportunity at hand and who in the agency
ll support the pursuit. Once you map all of the stakeholders, you can
e in a picture, who matters to your pursuit. If you don't know them, and
u work for a large company, you may have a legislative liaison in your
mpany who can make the connection with a legislative member who
s a vested interest in your opportunity pursuit. Following is an example
' a stakeholder map. Our fictitious solicitation has to do with
nsolidating all of Housing and Urban Development (HUD) datacenters
to a single datacenter hosted at Stennis Space Center in Hancock
ounty, Mississippi. Here is an example of what the stakeholder map
ight actually look like.

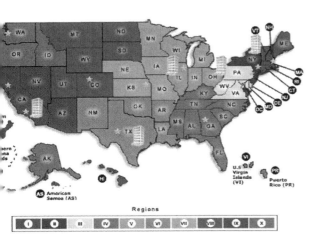

Let's begin by taking a look at what HUD's regional structure looks like. Note that MS is located in Region 4. This helps identify potential regional HUD

ersonalities with whom you may be interfacing.

ext, you want to identify State and Local Representatives whose
nstituency will be impacted by the datacenter consolidation activity.

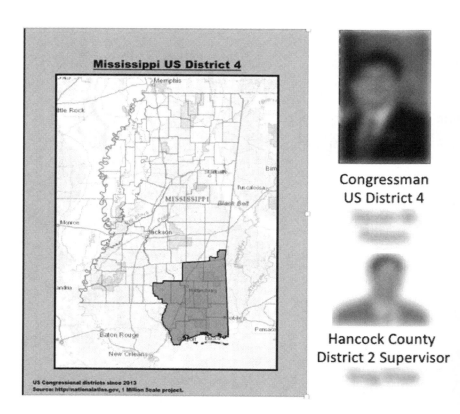

Congressman
US District 4

Hancock County
District 2 Supervisor

Here we have identified the congressman for the district and th county supervisor for Hancock County. These two are keenl interested in the success of the program as it will bring jobs and ta revenue to their districts, stimulating the local economy. Also, it i wise to know who represents this district in both the U.S. Senate an the House of Representatives. A total of six legislative individual represent Mississippi, two Senators, and four members of Congress.

Mississippi Senators & Representatives

Senior Senator

1st District

3rd District

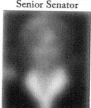

Junior Senator

2nd District

4th District

For the most part, these six legislative members will act on behalf of their constituency. They can be powerful allies in ensuring that a solicitation with this much economic impact is financially supported. Discover who comprises the United States Senate Banking Subcommittee on Housing, Transportation, and Community Development. This subcommittee has jurisdiction over the following:

- Urban mass transit, urban affairs and development
- Federal Transit Administration
- HUD
- Affordable Housing
- Foreclosure Mitigation
- Mortgage Servicing
- HAMP
- FHA
- Senior Housing
- Nursing home construction
- Rural Housing Service
- Indian Housing

Take note to both the Senate majority and minority members as th
may have different agendas that can impact the acquisition.

Such a Stakeholder Map can be created for any opportunity by simp
going online and looking up the senators, congressmen, state and loc
delegates, agency offices who have interests in mission, jobs, taxes ar
other benefits of having a large data center or retail store like Amazo
or other major win in their jurisdiction. Remember, they are lookir
out for the interest of the people in their jurisdictions. Therefore, th
will have strong interest in any decision that will benefit them ar
their constituents.

Turn your attention back to the agency, in this case, HUD. In tl
Challenges chapter, we discuss the typical structure within an agenc
Now it's time to identify those who are in each of those position
Identify the Secretary or Administrator and their appointed Deputy

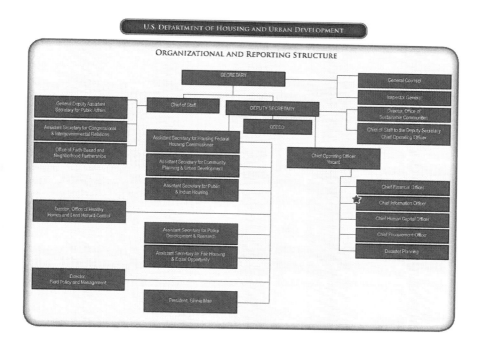

At HUD, the Chief Information Officer reports through the Chief Operating Officer to the Deputy Secretary. Go online and lookup who each personality is. Please copy and paste their professional pictures and organize your data to recognize the name and face of each executive.

Drill down into the Chief Information Officer's office and begin to identify key stakeholders within the organization that will have a direct impact on the solicitation.

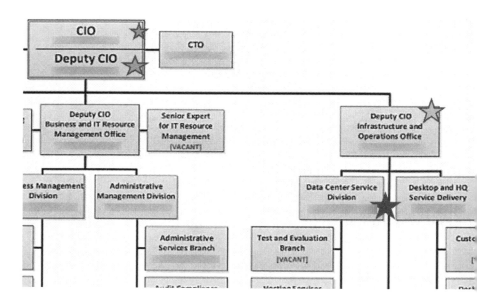

Note that there is a chain of authority from the CIO through the Depu
CIO Infrastructure and Operations Office to the Director for Da
Center Service Division. Again, put names to faces, find out where the
might be speaking and get to know their stake in the acquisition. Late
we will discuss how to connect to individuals, develop a call pla
determine each person's impact level, and execute successful engagement

Why Meet the CXO

have often been asked "Why is it even necessary to meet a Chief nformation Officer or Chief Financial Officer?" and, "Why would I need o know a customer executive?" One business development professional aid to me, "Chief Information Officers are so mean! I don't understand vhy I need to get to know them anyway. I can get the information about a project from the project manager."

There is tremendous frustration wrapped in these sorts of questions. Let's start with the statement concerning CIO's being "mean." Understand that executives are extremely busy in their day-to-day activities. They cannot afford to waste time in meetings that have no real purpose, are not planned, and do not result in something positive for the agency. Time is a valuable commodity for the government executive.

Many business developers only focus on their own needs and their own questions. They often do not consider that the person with whom they are meeting needs to gain a positive benefit from the meeting as well. Often times, the business developer will start the session asking the executive to do their homework for them. The business developer will whip out a PowerPoint presentation telling the executive all about their company, who their customers are, how big the company is, what their products and services are, and never try to understand what the customer

39

is interested in or what needs they have. Imagine how you feel when
telemarketer calls you trying to sell you something that you ha
absolutely no interest in. Whatever their solution is, it does not answ
the problems the executive is dealing with daily. Executives feel frustrat
when companies meet with them without any discussion to validate the
need before jumping into a proposed solution.

Recognize that I said "validate" their needs – not ask them to tell you wh
their needs are. So often, business developers want to escape th
homework they are required to do and just ask the customer to do it f
them. That is why customers seem annoyed at the meeting. They kno
that you are wasting their time when you come unprepared to help the
with their problems. We focus more on doing your research and preparir
to meet the customer, later in the book.

Why then is it important to meet with the customer executive? There a
several reasons!

To Gain a Better Understanding of the Environment

It is imperative to know your customer's work environment. You nee
to understand their mission, their goals, what is important to then
The more you know about the customer's situation, the mo
beneficial the conversations will be, the more credence the custome

will place in you, and the better able you are to understand their needs and how you can provide the ideal solution.

When working for one of the Fortune 50 firms, I was required to actually work in my customer's environment. I worked behind the scenes for 3 months to gain a full understanding of their work environment, how they delivered their outcomes to their customers, and really know how to communicate effectively with them about their business. By doing so, I became a trusted partner with them, and they saw me not as a vendor, but as one of them, understanding their pain, their needs, their ambitions, their customers, and what they really wanted to accomplish. I know this kind of activity is not readily afforded to business developers today. However, you can still learn about your customers on your own by doing your research and learning more about the customer environment.

Executives have knowledge about the entire environment, not just the small area of interest that your product or service may address. This is important because customers want to know how to solve their problems with total solutions, not just partial solutions being treated by one tool, product, or service. They think all day about the overall problem. And most importantly, they budget to address the total solution.

Gaining a Better Understanding of Business Priorities

The executive customer also sets the priorities for how problems w
be addressed. If you, as the business developer, do not understand ho
the problem you are trying to solve is prioritized, you may find th
you are pursuing an issue that is at the bottom of the priority list. No
that the budget will go towards the problems that are at the top of tl
customer priority list. Although the people at the lower levels in tl
organization can tell you a lot of detail about the projects you a
interested in, they do not always know how any project is prioritize
in the grand scheme of things. The result can be that you sper
countless days and months pursuing a perceived opportunity just 1
have the rug pulled out from under you because the project was not
priority in the organization.

If you discover that the project you are interested in does not meet tl
criteria for being a top priority in the organization, you still hav
options. Dialogue with the executive about why it should be essenti
to the organization if they do not treat the project as a high priorit
Align the project to some other top priority. Healthy dialogue an
alignment can drastically increase your chances of winning the wor
to address the newly prioritized need.

The customer will budget money for their priorities. In corporat
America, corporate executives know the customer's core prioritie

setting tactical activity for the business development workforce. All the employees of the company are governed by these priorities and strategies. In comparison to government, Federal Executives do the same and all employees SHOULD follow suit.

The business developer must know what the agency's priorities are, and the best place to learn this is from customer leadership. Remember, lower-level employees in the organization cannot set these priorities, nor can they change them. They can, however, offer you a lot of detailed information about the operations and the details of the problems they face. Therefore, it is crucial to know the customer at the executive, program, and project levels. As recent as within the past six months prior to the publishing of this book, I worked with a client who spent an enormous amount of time and money pursuing an opportunity. They had not met with the decision makers and were confident that their experience in the solution area they were presenting would win them the business. By the time my client requested my involvement, it was too late. The project was defunded and all of their work was in vain.

Gaining a Better Understanding of the Budget

Once the priorities are established, and the budget is formulated, the money is spent on those priorities. The project-level employees then receive their budgets to execute their projects. But they never know when a project may be de-funded because it is no longer a priority at the executive level. Funding can be re-directed to another project that is now more important. I was personally involved in decisions to re route budget dollars as a Department-level CIO and know how th works firsthand.

If you have established that trust relationship with agency executiv leadership, you can openly converse with them on spend priorities an budgetary needs. That trust provides the necessary foundation t discuss and consider impacts on the anticipated goals of the agency Sometimes, another point of view has convinced leadership t reestablish budgets.

> **Note:** When a customer tells you that they have no money that is not necessarily true. It simply means that YOU hav not convinced them that they NEED to spend money on th solutions you are providing.

Access to Other CXO's in Other Organizations

Still, another reason to get to know the executives is that when yo convince them that you really can help solve their problems, they wil introduce you across the enterprise. They will want their colleagues t know that there, indeed, is an available fix to the issues, and they wi want to garner the support of their peers. They will also want to mak sure that targeted executives with similar difficulties have access to th best solution for the good of the organization. The executive will begin to introduce you to their colleagues in the other agencies and industry partners, where they believe your ideas and solutions can be beneficial.

There were many times that I, as a Chief Information Officer (CIO), would introduce a particular company to the assistant secretaries, directors, and others who could benefit from what the company was offering. I would also introduce, over lunch or dinner, which is always optimal, the business developer to other CIOs in other agencies who I knew faced the same challenges I faced. We enjoyed a camaraderie and would always try to help each other out when we could. At the Federal CIO Council level, we were continually trying to solve universal CIO/agency problems. I would introduce the ideas being presented to me if I genuinely believed in them. This opened many doors for the business developer that he/she could not have opened on their own.

want to reiterate the importance of getting to know agency executives or CXO's. Be sure you read the rest of the book to understand how to do our homework and prepare for such a meeting. You may only get one hance to make a lasting impression. BE PREPARED!!!

Now that we know who to know, let's talk about how to build elationships with those individuals.

Relationship building

Many average business developers think that customers buy from them their company simply because of the product's brand they are sellin They sometimes believe that the customer will buy from them because the "name" of the company for which they are currently working. In n consulting role, I have had customers tell me to let my industry clie know that they will not do business with them unless they remove particular business developer from the account. No matter whether the customer is commercial, federal, state, or local governmen RELATIONSHIPS are critical to making the sale.

Excellent business developers understand that relationships are critical making a sale and continuing a business relationship with a customer for years to come. Pros also understand how a significant relationship with their customer may result in an introduction to other potential custome within the agency. I have also experienced an introduction opportunities outside the agency with whom we were doing business, du to that well-established trust relationship. Since relationships are essential, let's explore how we build and maintain those relationships.

Tips on Relationship Building

When building relationships with anyone – not just customers - the are certain things that you must always consider:

Above all else, *be yourself*. A person can tell when you are trying to be something or someone you are not. If you start out building relationships under false pretenses, the truth will come out eventually, and you will appear to the customer as being deceitful and not trustworthy. When you connect with a person on similar values, beliefs, and personality, the relationship can accelerate rather than deteriorate because of false assumptions.

Mutual respect is, likewise, a critical factor in building relationships. It takes time to build trust with another person. You both are observing each other's actions and listening to beliefs and values. If all those things are in synch, eventually, you build a mutual trust which can last forever.

Identify *mutual goals and values* that foster trust and respect needed for a favorable and beneficial relationship.

Also, help those with whom you want to establish relationships to build relationships with others. Can you support them in building a desired relationship? *Help them network*, and they will be very grateful to you for helping them move their objectives and careers along.

Let them know that *you are human* and that you make mistakes too! This ties to being your authentic self as we just discussed. Careful with this! It would be best if you read your audience before showing vulnerabilities and be very careful about what weakness you share. *A* you slowly begin to relax around them, they will also start to rel around you. Eventually, you will enter into an exchange of person thoughts about a topic or shared vulnerability.

Show loyalty to the person with whom you are trying to build relationship; discretion with personal information shows integrity ar can be a tight rope to walk. Don't tattle on people within th customer's organization to endear yourself. If you are forced in discussing staff issues, provide input as to specific directions that w help the team succeed. Above all, never talk about customers behir their backs or side publicly against them. It would be best if yc showed loyalty, even when you disagree. If you disagree with them c a matter, take it up with them in private and always provide a solutio:

Plan personal time together. It is important to get out of the office ar into an environment where you both can relax. Spending tin together away from the office will go a long way towards building healthy relationship. You could go to dinner, lunch, a ball gam festival, or any other event of mutual interest. When you are awa from the office, you learn more about the person, their family, the interests, experiences, ideas, and points of view. They, in turn, wi discover the same things about you.

Don't establish unreal expectations about the person with whom you want to build a relationship. As you learn more about the person, expectations between the two of you will develop naturally. Too soon, and you will set each other up for disappointment. If you find your customer is struggling with some issue, brainstorm alongside them to find an answer. Partnering without expecting something in return builds trust and credibility.

Never ask for something from the customer until you have been able to offer something to him/her. It may be a connection to someone they need to get to know, an introduction to a physician that they are in search of, a scholarship program for their child, a real estate agent that is very good, and other things like this that may be of help. After you have helped them with something important, then you might find yourself in a position to ask for something from them. I am not talking about bartering; this is making sure the relationship is mutually "give and take" and never one-sided.

Tracking Relationships

Parker Group Consulting has developed a relationship-tracking methodology that has been used successfully at several large corporations. It is called "Relationship Tracker." The method has seven levels of relationships, as depicted on the next page:

Level 0	*Name Only*
	0 – 1 Months
	• Knows the name

Level 1	*Face Only*
	0 – 3 Months
	• Can associate a name with the face
	• Maybe have seen the person at an event, on television or in the press

Level 2	*Acquaintance*
	2 – 12 Months
	• Has met with the person at least 2 times – in the company of others or alone on some support topic

Level 3	*Business Respect*
	6 – 15 Months
	• Has been called in to meet with the person on a topic important to the person; initiated by the person

Level 4	*Trusted Vendor*
	6 – 24 Months
	• Has accepted an invitation from you to an event at least twice
	• Has asked you for a white paper on a subject which they are trying to understand
	• Called back within 24 – 48 hours after leaving a message
	• Reaches out after a meeting (within a week) to advise on an issue
	• Asked you to attend a staff meeting to explain/address a solution to a business problem

Level 5	*Business Friend*
	12 – 36 Months
	• Has invited you to an event (Conference tag-up, drinks, Holiday Party, etc) at least twice, whether business or personal
	• Has called you to forewarn you of a contract action/ activity/ opportunity/ other vendor activity
	• Has introduced you to two or more of his/her colleagues
	• Actively supported you in a business opportunity to at least two of his/her colleagues by vouching for your solution and giving you advice on how to proceed with their colleague.
	• Provided his/her colleague with reasons why they think your solution is best either in writing or verbally with or without your presence
	• Keeps you informed of career moves ahead of the press

Level 6	*Personal Friend*
	18 – 36 Months
	• Relationship has become a friendship with cell phone numbers exchanged and ability to talk on weekends
	• Invitation to kids' events including sports and concerts, sends holiday greetings, invites you to personal holiday parties
	• Attends sporting events with you
	• Keeps in touch with you on any career moves

At level 0, you only *know the person's name*, maybe in a news article, an announcement, or on some organization chart. Someone may have mentioned their name to you as someone moving into a position of importance that you need to get to know.

At level 1, you have *associated the name with a face.* Maybe you have seen the person in the news, on television, on stage at a conference, or in passing. Someone may have pointed the person out to you.

Level 2 is the beginning of the work in *establishing a relationship*. At this point, you may have been in a meeting with the person with whom you want to develop the relationship. You may have been introduced at a function and had a chance to say a few words to the person. CAREFUL HERE! NEVER use an informal introduction at an event to start your sales pitch. A sales pitch at this level is a BIG TURNOFF! There is a time for that! At this stage, you are just an acquaintance. The customer does not know you and probably will not remember your name. Make their first experience with you, your name, and your face non-threatening and pleasant. You may have several "level 2" encounters with your customer. You want each to be an enjoyable experience. At some point, and again briefly, share your prepared elevator speech, appreciating their issues, identifying how you solved that problem elsewhere, quantify the successful experience

and ask for a quick meeting to discuss how you can do the same f
them.

Level 3 is the level where you have established *business respect* with th
customer. During level 2 encounters, maybe through your elevat
speech or open comments in conversation, you convinced th
customer that you are knowledgeable and can be helpful. At this poin
the customer has called on you to meet with him/her. Do not b
surprised if the customer's team players are present to maximize th
outcomes. The meeting is scheduled with you because yo
knowledge is respected, and the customer has taken notice.

Level 4 is the place in the relationship that defines you to the custom
as a *trusted vendor*. At this level, the customer has shown trust in yo
and your knowledge. The customer views you as a problem solver an
will begin calling you to clarify his/her thinking further. They wi
return your phone calls right away because they know that you hav
something valuable to offer, trusting your judgment. At this poin
they recognize that you will not waste their time.

At *level 5*, you are a *business friend*. Your relationship has mature
such that the customer is asking you to join him/her on outings, fo
lunch, to meet up at conferences, and other events. A friendship ha
developed where the customer makes sure you know when he/she i
moving from one position to another. You are invited to th

celebrations, have their new contact information and your friend ensures their new staff knows who you are. They will also introduce you to others in other departments and even in other agencies or companies. They will vouch for you, your history in providing support and a dependable solution, and promote you as a valuable partner.

Finally, the highest *level is 6 - Personal Friend*. At this level, you have the customer's private email address, phone number, and cell phone. They invite you into their family world. The customer asks you to holiday parties and personal events involving their families, such as graduations, ball games, or other activities of a private nature. You have entered their inside friend circles. You have indeed become a real friend.

Which level is appropriate?

You will need to determine which level makes sense for you and the customer with whom you are building the relationship. These relationship levels take many months and years to build, and you cannot wait for level 6 to begin to do business with this customer. But you can continue to build the relationship to the degree that you think is sufficient for you and your customer's objectives. You are not building these relationships to use people. That is far from the case. You should always keep in mind that you are building a two-way, mutual relationship. We build relationships every day outside of

business, and in a healthy relationship, both parties bene
tremendously. Otherwise, there is no real relationship. Determi
what level you want to achieve and put your plan in place to g
through the levels. It may not even be noticeable to you that th
relationship is building, so you need to track it. Below is an examp
tracker sheet for use in tracking your relationship levels by client.

Name, Title	Level/Date						
	0	1	2	3	4	5	6
Joe Smith, CIO		12/27					

How do you verify that you have reached each level?

1. Column 1 - List the name, title, and agency/company (
   the person with whom you want to you want to build
   relationship
2. Columns 2-7 – Upon completion of any of the activities i
   the relationship description sheet, check the box in th
   column corresponding to the customer's name and plac
   the date that you achieved the level next to the checkmar
   (see example on sheet)
3. Continue this process until you reach the desire
   relationship level
4. Attach any supporting documentation; invitations, reque
   for whitepapers, commendations, etc.
5. Review your tracker sheet quarterly with your manager

The Mindset to Connect with a Customer Executive

I have often had customers ask me why is it that CXO's are so difficult to connect with. I hear comments like, "The CIO never wants to hear what I have to say", "The CIO seems so uninterested in what I am presenting" and "I am never invited back".

In this chapter we will discuss what you can do to reinvent your approach in order to captivate the CXO or Key Customer! You must transform yourself into a Trusted Partner, rather than a peddler! First thing you need to understand is what is it that will captivate the CXO!

Understanding the Current Issues

It is so vital that you understand both the current issues facing the executive of the organization and the overall priorities and challenges of the organization. The organization takes direction from multiple sources. One source is congress, who appropriates the money to carry out the mission of the department. The congressmen always have their constituents in mind, so they will weigh in to ensure that the budgets support their priorities. They will often issue mandates to the agencies, some of which are funded while others are not funded. Mandates also come directly from the White House. These mandates are based upon the President's priorities and his/her agenda.

An excellent example of this phenomenon is the argument over tl border wall, which was directed but unfunded. The debate is center on the funding of the wall. Budget line items associated with oth projects and priorities have been pulled and re-routed to the bord wall. This fight has involved the White House (or Executive Brancl the Legislative Branch, and even the Judiciary Branch. Monies th many large contractors thought were going to be used on their projec are being re-directed in support of the president's priority. Althoug this is typically much larger than the preferences you may be workir on, it is essential to understand that mandates from Congress, tl White House, and the Judiciary branch can circumvent you marketing efforts. These priorities can change the budget that yc have been planning your efforts around.

Agencies may also be dealing with other cost issues associated wit overspending their budgets requiring decision-makers to cut back c some of the projects they had planned to undertake. They may hav projects that are "hemorrhaging" money and costing more than tl agency expected. If the project is a top priority, this can obviously caus a reduction in the availability of funds allocated towards other projec or programs.

One example of overspending occurred at one of the federal agencie where I served. The Secretary wanted to implement a new custome service initiative, which required the hiring of 600 new employees t be stationed around the country for the new outreach program. Without checking into the feasibility of the budget to accommodate this initiative, the human resources team, trying to satisfy the desires and priorities of the Secretary, quickly hired 600 people. Turns out, there was no budget for them. The agency came under fire from Congress, and there was much talk about requiring all agency employees to be furloughed for a few days out of the year to save money to pay for the new hires. Needless to say, this was not a popular solution. After much debate, the money was eventually allocated by Congress on an emergency basis to pay for the new hires. Several people lost their jobs over this issue. What's important to learn from this story is that budgets can change, and spending can be out of control. It is essential for you, as a business developer, to have your hand on the pulse and know when these kinds of actions can impact your marketing plans.

There are also transformation issues plaguing government today. Federal organizations are trying to transform the way they do business and to be more efficient and to serve their customers and citizens better. They have been directed to become more citizen-centric and to transform their technologies to take advantage of cost reductions in the more efficient technologies of today. They have been directed to stop over-spending on high maintenance systems and to use new technologies like – "cloud technologies" and Mobile apps - to provide better services to the citizens and customers at a reduced cost.

Substantial funding has been allocated to transformation efforts, ar business developers need to understand how their solutions fit into tl transformation strategies. Recognizing this can help justify how tl dollars set aside for transformation can be used for the solutions y(are trying to provide.

Other issues that warrant your attention that agencies are facir include but are not limited to;

- Cybersecurity issues which today have substantial budg allocations,
- Centers of Excellence which have become an administratic priority to ensure more efficiencies and better custom service,
- Waste, fraud, and abuse issues that the Investigator Gener (IG), and the Government Accountability Office (GAO) a focusing on   to ensure agency accountability and elimina waste.

We will cover how to research and identify these issues later. For no let's discuss how to build your solution to address your custome problems.

Your Solution

First and foremost, your solution must SOLVE a high priority problem for the customer. Keep in mind that your customer thinks about his/her agency dilemmas every day, and they are tasked to solve those problems. Your solution must be a COMPLETE solution to the issue. Many business developers work to get in to see the customer with little or no knowledge of these issues the customer is facing and what priorities they are focusing their energies on. Average to poor business developers want to get in to sell a widget. They are only prepared to talk about one product or service when the customer is thinking about a much larger predicament that requires a complete solution. When you go in selling a widget, the customer is turned off because you are only focused on your widget, which only provides a "part" of the solution or no part of the solution at all. It becomes clear to the customer that this meeting is "all about you".

Consider the following examples of this problematic approach to selling. First, suppose you are having a big party, and you need to plan the food, fun, music, decorations. One party planner comes to meet with you and tells you that they can take care of the decorations. You are still burdened with trying to figure out all the other elements to make the party a success. A second party planner provides services that address all four requirements. Your preference and attention will go to the planner who comes in and tells you that they can take care

of the whole thing. It doesn't matter to you that the planner inten
on using other providers to ensure the desired outcome. Second
consider building a house. You meet with a contractor who tells y
that he/she can provide you with the best floors on earth, but that
it. Another general contractor tells you that they can build the who
house and will manage all the partners that will deliver the wal
floors, roof, exterior, landscaping, etc. Which contractor will you wa
to spend time with? Understand that when you are meeting with
potential customer that they are focused on the problem in its entire
not just what your widget will do.

That customer will also want to learn from you what the best optio
are. When you approach them as an expert, they will begin to trust y
and lean on you for sound advice. Remember that contractor you hir
to build your house? You are going to trust the one that can give y
expert advice on what needs to be done and who can bring the be
contractors to the table to complete the job. The same holds true
our marketplace. The customer will trust and want to work with t
business developer/company that they can learn from. They belie
that you can bring the right people to the table to make the
successful.

Another story I can tell to solidify the point is my own house-buildir
experience. While living in North Carolina, I built a house from t
ground up. The builder (general contractor) was awful! I had to g

to the house every day to check behind him and every day I uncovered another problem. I'd have to go to the builder to complain and in every situation, they would have to tear out what they had done and redo it. They had to re-landscape and they had to tear down ceilings and walls and redo. It was a horrible experience for me. When we moved to Maryland, again, we started building a house from scratch. I was very stressed out because I just knew that I was going to have the same problems with the Maryland builder. I would show up at the house every day to find the problems to point out to him. Much to my surprise, I never found an issue. One evening, I went by and saw that an upstairs wall was crooked. When I went back to the site the next morning to catch the builder, he walked into the house with me and I did not see the crookedness in the wall. He asked, "Was it the wall you were concerned about?" I said "yes" and he said, "I saw that on my morning inspection and directed the team to do it over." I was stunned but extremely happy. I reached the point where I totally trusted the builder and stopped taking all of my time trying to check behind him. I am still in the house today after 30 years and have never had a problem with his work. I recommended him to everybody I knew! That is the kind of relationship and trust you want your customer to have in you and your company.

Also consider that a complete solution may require partners. It is prudent to meet with potential partners who can help you solve the entire problem. Learn how their solution can complement what you

are bringing to the table. Once you've done this essential homewo:
the customer will view you as the teacher, the expert, the one they ne
on their team. NOT the widget salesman! Otherwise, other compan
who do their homework well will be favored over you.

Differentiate yourself

I have listened to many business developers from both small and la:
businesses make the statement that their solution (products a
services) are just like everybody else's. "Company A has an equival
product" or "Company B can provide the exact same services." If t
is their thought process - that they are the same as everybody els
why should the potential customer want to do business with them
successful business cannot just be like everybody else. They m
differentiate their company, products, and services to lead the pac
have always referred to this phenomenon as the "wolf pack." We
know that when wolves are hunting as a pack, there exists an al
wolf. The Alpha always gets to the prey and eats FIRST!! Otl
within the pack get whatever is left over if anything. The best busi:
development pros always strive to be the alpha wolf. That wolf
differentiated itself with strength, wisdom, intellect, skills, prow
courage, and determination. Most followers get what is left, and s
don't get anything at all. Differentiate yourself, i.e., your company
solution with differentiation options. Let's review what some of tl
might be:

Function – It may be that the feature that your solution provides is unique. No other company offers it, or no other company's solution is as robust as yours. Understand the functions of your offering and compare it to your competitors. Determine whether or not this is your differentiator.

Price – It may be that the functions are the same, but your price is lower. Or your solution offers more functionality at the same rate as your competitor, who may not provide as much. Understand the price comparisons and know if that is your differentiator.

Skills – What about the skill levels of your company's employees? Maybe their skill levels are higher than your competitors. Maybe your people have more certifications, more training, more time working on a specific solution. Maybe you have unique skills, such as COBOL to assist the transformation from a legacy system to new innovative technologies. Is skill level your differentiator?

Management – How about your management team? I always looked to see how many layers I had to go through to get to a high-ranking executive who could make sure my project was implemented successfully. In some companies, the management team is visible, and they build relationships with customer executives. In some companies, they sit on a high pedestal and never come out to meet the customer unless they are forced 1 Customers desire to know that the management team is involv and working to ensure success. This is an exception differentiator.

Value – It may be that your solution delivers the best value comparison to the competitive landscape. Do you bring more the table for the money being spent? Evaluate your cost and serv offering. Compare your worth against your competito Determine how to return the best value, then articulate that your customer.

Experience – Determine if your firm has greater depth, skill, a knowledge than the competition. Your past performance r demonstrate that your company has satisfied the sa requirement for more clients with high customer satisfaction. C example of this might be that your company has more exposur Customer Experience solutions such as Amazon, Nordstre banking, and others. Other companies competing for this typ business have only worked in a smaller setting without as m depth. Leverage your company's experience and past performa as a significant differentiator.

Innovation – Identify areas of unique innovation that set y solution apart from the competition. Learn how to articulate research, design, technology selection, implementation, and integration strategies that got your customer(s) a "win."

Quality – Maybe your company's quality processes are the best in the industry, and your products are proven to be less likely to fail. If this is your differentiation, use it!

In his book, In Pursuit – Business Development Life Cycle, Mike Rice states, "*When I recognize a discriminator, I asked that tough question again, "So What?". If my solution is "blue" and my competition is "red," determine whether or not the color blue means anything. If it's not a discriminator, it's not; and not part of my messaging.*"[12] I agree with his statement. Determine what is essential to your customer and send that message.

You must set yourself and your company apart from the rest of the pack. If you and your company are the same as all the others, why should an executive or critical customer spend their valuable time talking to you? Make sure you are different, the best value, more skilled, more experienced, more innovative, higher in quality, and overall, the best choice for success. Make sure you are the "Alpha" wolf!

Rice, Mike. *In Pursuit – Business Development Life Cycle*. CornerStone IT, LLC. ©2019

How to Research for the Meeting with CXO

The most effective business developers know their customers' needs, the plans, their budgets, their priorities, their justifications for spending. T business developer also knows the competitive landscape. Seasoned pr know who to talk to, who the decision-makers are, who the influence are, who their foes are, who in the account can provide the be information on strategy and priorities, and who can provide the be information on infrastructure and technical details. A GREAT busine developer NEVER ASKS THE CUSTOMER TO DO THE1 RESEARCH FOR THEM! That is one of the biggest "turnoffs" for a: customer. They have their work to do and are not pleased to do the wo of the business developer also! Approaching a busy customer, unprepare is NOT a pleasant experience for them, at all! As a prepared profession the customer sees you as an expert, and is more impressed with yo knowledge! You become the person they want to spend time meeting.

RESEARCH is critical – DO YOUR HOMEWORK

Let's talk about how to do the research.

There are many ways and many resources to utilize to get yo homework done. Here are a few suggestions that have worked for n in the past:

Event Attendance

Attend events where the customer is speaking. Be sure to have a prepared "Elevator Speech" in case you have an opportunity to approach the customer. There are specific rules of engagement. NEVER monopolize the customer's time. They are not there for you to conduct a sales call. They are there to speak and meet new colleagues or network with existing colleagues. Monopolizing their time is disrespectful to other event attendees who are trying to meet the customer just like you. This practice is incredibly annoying and disconcerting to the customer. They typically are glancing around trying to figure out how to get away from an overbearing business developer. They will not forget any lousy experience. Future meetings will be difficult to secure as they will attempt to avoid overbearing business developers. I am stating these facts from personal experience as a customer executive.

When attending these events, make sure you listen carefully and ask intelligent questions. Again, demonstrate that you are an expert and have done your homework. You will distinguish yourself that way. Listen intently to what they are describing as their hot buttons and needs. An event is one of the best places to learn what is on a customer's mind. At the end of the presentation, introduce yourself to the customer with a well-developed "elevator speech." You will more likely establish a

one-on-one meeting if you execute your introducti?
correctly.

When I used to speak as the Chief Information Officer o?
federal agency, I would always have many people line up to ?
to meet me and give me their business cards or corpor?
brochures. I remember that at one event, 25 people were lin?
up after a breakfast meeting to talk to me. Each one would st?
up on their turn in line and would say, "Hi! My name is Jo?
Smith, and I would like to come to meet with you to tell y?
about my product/service! When can I get on your calendar?
Truthfully, I had no desire to meet with this person. I was?
interested in their product or their solution. They did n?
relate to our dilemma, did not do their homework, a?
approached me with what I expected as a corporate capabiliti?
pitch. I would respectfully take their business card and t?
them I would get back to them while looking beyond them ?
the next person. After about ten people, one would step up a?
say, "Hi, my name is Jane Doe, and I thought your words tod?
were captivating. I learned that you have a dire need to redu?
your maintenance costs on your legacy systems a?
significantly enhance customer productivity and satisfacti?
with these systems that support your critical mission. ?
accomplished your exact objective at the XYZ agency. Th?
reduced their costs by 50% and increased customer satisfacti?

by 45% to 97%. They also saw productivity increases in the program staff of nearly 75%. I would appreciate some time to talk to you about how we can help you accomplish very similar results." Wow! What an elevator pitch. Well researched and well-tuned to what I needed to hear. Only took 30 seconds! I took this person's card, make a mark on it, and ensured her that I would be in touch. This process continued through the entire 25 people in line, and only two cards ended up with a mark made by me (secretly). When I got back to the office, I gave the business cards to my administrative assistant, and she would call the two that had been marked and set up meetings. Now that was a successful event for both my new industry partner and me.

Join Industry Associations

Identify and join the associations in the industry with which you are associated. Don't just join, take an active role in the organization, and engage in their activities. Frankly, this is another venue to meet key customers and find yourself invited to the events where they are speaking. You may get the opportunity to work side-by-side with that customer you want to get to know. Mostly because they are members of the same organizations, and they, too, volunteer their time on targeted committees. Working together on a project is an excellent way

to get to know them and build the kind of relationship y(
desire. Identify the associations that are the best in yo
industry, read your industry magazines, and look at tl
conferences that are coming up. That is a great way to lea
about the associations. Your company will also have tl
opportunity to sponsor some of the events of the associatic
and get the company name promoted to people who have a
interest.

Some examples of associations in the Technology Industry a
AFFIRM (Association for Federal Information Resour(
Management), ACT/IAC (American Council c
Technology/Industry Advisory Council), ATARC (Advance
Technology Academic Research Center; formerly known
GITEC), AFCEA (Air Force Communications Executi
Association), PSC (Professional Services Council), and othe

Subscribe to research organizations

Subscribe to research organizations to learn wh
agencies/companies are saying their needs are, their success(
are, their forecasts, and their budgets. Research organizatio1
reach out to agencies/companies on opportunities ar
budgets, publishing the information so that companies kno
which opportunities to pursue. Examples of these researc
organizations include the Professional Services Counc

Gartner, Bloomberg, Forrester, and others, in the public and private technology industry. There is also GovWin and FedBizOps, where the business development professional can research up and coming acquisitions. Your company probably has a corporate membership for many of these research organizations. I have spoken to many business developers who did not know that they had access to this type of information. It appears that some companies make these memberships available to their internal sales forces but not to the business development people in the field. Don't be afraid to ask for access. After all, your company is paying for it to help increase their business posture. If your company does not have access to these research firm documents, do your research on them and sell the idea of membership to your company. It will help both the internal sales force, the executives, and the business development teams.

Subscribe to Trade Journals.

Read about all the issues and news in your industry. Many CXO's and other vital customer roles provide interviews for articles in the trade journals. Trade publications provide a great way to keep up with current hot issues in the industry. In the public and private technology landscape, several of these trade journals include CIO Magazine, Federal Computer Week,

Government Executive Magazine, and others. There are al
newsletters that you can subscribe to in your industry, as we
as social media, articles, and blogs. Many executives today w
write blogs and post information on Facebook and particular
in LinkedIn so that you can connect to them, listen to ar
understand their needs and thoughts, and learn directly fro
them.

Employees in the agency or company

Talk to employees in the agencies and companies where yo
want to do business. Even if you think they are not associate
with your area of interest, they may know the people you wai
to know and may have some insight that can help you find tl
information you are in search of. In the call plan discussio
we talk about the people you will want to meet. They a
decision-makers, influencers, knowledge resources, ar
friends. They are all employees of the agency or compan
Figure out which ones can help you based upon what you a
trying to achieve and talk to them to gain knowledge ar
access. Depending on the level of the contact you make, the
can generally fill you in on a lot about the issues in the agen
and the priorities established by the leadership of the agenc
They can also introduce you to the very people with whom yo
need to speak. Never discount individual contacts simp

because of their rank. You never know, they may have access to those you need to engage.

Talk to other companies.

Although this may sound a little far-fetched, I see business developers who do this very well. They talk to other companies about what is going on in a particular account or customer environment. They find out more about what is happening in the accounts where they have interests just by talking to other companies – even competitors. There is one business developer that I regard as one of the best in the industry. She has an incredible knack for getting other companies to let her know the status of opportunities. She knows what's hot in the agency and which competitors are going after which bids. She can tell you what the customer thinks of specific companies. She knows when procurements are scheduled, current budgets for a particular project, and so much more. I am always amazed when she calls me to give me the latest on an opportunity. I then assume, due to the depth of her understanding that she got the information directly from the agency. Then, once again, I am amazed to find out that she acquired all that intel from her competitor just merely by calling and asking them what they know. This knack of hers puts her in a unique position to identify critical teaming partners. Sometimes, if you are not competing with them, they are more than willi

to give you a ton of information about the competiti

landscape.

Customer's Website

One continuously overlooked source of information is t

customer's website. Take the time to review the agency

mission, strategic plan, offices of operation, budget, forecas

and many other areas of interest found directly from the

public facing website. The agencies will post all t

information they can about what they are working on, wh

their plans and priorities are, and who the key players a

Please read the articles that they post on their website. Agen

web media can also afford you a considerable amount

insight into what is important to them.

Federal Budget and other Office of Management and Budget Informatic

The Office of Management and Budget is the administrati

arm of the White House in the Federal government. Th

handle finance, technology, and other administrative functio

of the Executive branch of government. For governme

agencies, be sure to read the federal budget. There is a ton

information in the United States Budget document on t

Office of Management and Budget website that speaks to h

the budget was justified and what the priorities of the government agency are. You can also find all the agency justifications for the budget requests in OMB documents that used to be called Exhibit 53 (Agency IT Portfolio) and Exhibit 300 (Capital Asset Plan and Business Case Summary). Also, for government agencies, you can read the agency's IG (Inspector General's) findings on the agency. This document speaks to the inefficiencies of the agency and what they need to improve. Likewise, the GAO (General Accounting Office) reports will offer great insight into the needs of the agency. It points out problems that the agency needs to correct. In both cases, both reports suggest ways in which the agency can correct sited deficiencies. It is essential to note that each agency must respond to these findings. You will get the benefit of seeing what solution the agency is planning to remediate the audit finding. By the way, these are key indicators of what a CXO's pain points might be.

Know How to Get a Meeting

There are so many business developers who struggle to understand he to get a meeting with the right customer. They pound the pavement tryi to knock on doors and that just does not work. We have discussed previous chapters how to gain the attention of a key customer and talk about the elevator speech. The elevator speech is used to gain immedi attention and is a very short attention-getter aimed at a customer's speci pain point. You only have one chance, particularly in a chance encount to make a great impression and gain the customer's desire to want to me There are some rules we'll discuss here that will prepare you for th meeting with the customer once you have secured it. There are also sor rules you must follow once the meeting is over to ensure that you ke your foot in the door. Let's discuss those points here.

Call Plan

Once you understand with whom you will need to build a relationsh it is vital to establish a call plan for that potential customer. There some aspects of a call plan that you must consider. Most call pla that I have seen merely state with whom the business developer war to meet, who will arrange the meeting, and the scheduled date of t meeting. There is so much more to a successful call plan.

It is imperative that a business developer thoroughly plan the meeti that benefits both the customer and your firm. It is the responsibil of the business developer to ensure the company comes out of the meeting with anticipated outcomes. To ensure a successful outcome, you must think through what you want to accomplish and how it will benefit both parties. The following represents core elements of a successful call plan:

Name	Position	Impact Level D,I,K,F	Objective	Message	Planned Outcome	Assigned To	When	Scheduled Date	Comments

D → Decision Maker
I → Influencer
K → Knowledge Resource
F → Friend

The first step is to determine with whom you need to talk to within the customer landscape. Typically, you are looking for a person who can support your objectives. Determine the role this person will play in the overall program? Is this a decision-maker? Your audience may not be the person who will ultimately make the decision but can influence the decision-maker. The point is that you really need to know whom you want to meet with and why!

I've said it before. I'm saying it now. And I will say it again. It is imperative to gain respect as a knowledgeable, well-prepared consultant that the customer believes has the acumen and experience to help them resolve their business problems. The reality is that you are there to solve, not sell. Take the time to learn more about their needs and challenges before meeting with them. Maybe find a mutual friend who knows this decision-maker or some other knowled resource in the account. Do your research!

It is necessary to determine the timing of each meeting, the purpo of the meeting, and the message. In his book, In Pursuit – Busine Development Life Cycle, Mike states, *"... align the appropriate tea member to take the appropriate message to the appropriate receiver of th message at the appropriate time. "Appropriate" is the "appropriate" word this discussion."*[13] I cannot agree more. For a specific call, you may ne to bring along someone who brings that acumen discussed abov someone who can address the customer's dilemma. A call with t customer can be more than one person. Caution, though, please lim attendees. (Don't pull up in the corporate bus with all seats filled! You do not want to overwhelm your audience and possibly stifle op or creative conversation.

On your call sheet, list the name and position of the person wi whom you plan to meet. List the level of support you expect to recei from that person. Is this a decision-maker, an influencer, a knowled resource, or a friend? Remember that each meeting will have its ow plan, its own objectives, and potentially its own participants. Ea row will reflect separate encounters with their own agenda's.

---

[13] Rice, Mike. In Pursuit – Business Development Life Cycle. CornerStone IT, LLC. ©2019

The next step is to plan the objective. What is the purpose of the meeting? Remember our Business Development Types? Type 1 - the "doing nothing" and the Type 2 - the "doing some." I can identify them immediately. I have tried to mentor some business developers only to hear them say to me, "I just need to meet with them because my management wants me to meet with someone in the account." These are hard to teach, produce no wins, and usually circulate in the BD landscape every 18 months or so doing the "BD dance". Meeting to meet is not a valid objective.

Also, when I ask the BD'er about their objective in setting up the meeting, they respond with, "I want to meet so that I can tell the customer about our capabilities." Once again, I warn them that they are headed for failure. KEY CUSTOMERS HATE TO HAVE A CAPABILITIES MEETING! I cannot emphasize that enough. Remember that a customer is not interested in you or your company's capabilities until they know that you understand their challenges and know how to help them. It is that motivation that develops the purpose of the meeting.

In the next chapter, we discuss the *Six Steps of a Successful Customer Meeting*. 1) How do I establish rapport? 2) How do I gain the customer's interest? 3) Make sure I fully understand the customer's needs. 4) Appropriately present the solution. At the very least, talk

about how you have solved the same problem elsewhere. 5) Prepare
handle objections appropriately. And finally, 6) close the meetin
asking for your planned outcomes—all great building blocks f
developing successful objectives. Later, you will learn how to execu
the objectives that you have set in the call plan. Don't forget to ta]
into consideration all objectives that are of interest to the customer.

An objective aligned precisely for the customer may be to understan
better how you solved similar problems elsewhere. Maybe yc
introduced some emerging technology, and the customer wants
learn about how you assessed, selected, implemented, and integrate
that solution. Some learning expeditions on behalf of the custom
can present tremendous opportunities to develop further objectiv
and planned outcomes.

For you, it may be to understand the customer's needs better and
validate what you have learned in your research. If you are furth
along in the conversations, you may be trying to get the customer
take a particular action, such as visiting a site to see the solution
work, or introducing you to the decision-maker and validating you
a trusted partner. There are many other objectives that you may con
up with, but you must take the time to plan the purpose of tl
meeting.

Once you know what your meeting objective will be, the next step is to craft your message to the customer. THE MESSAGE, EARLY IN THE PROCESS, WILL NOT BE TO TELL THE CUSTOMER WHAT YOUR COMPANY'S CAPABILITES ARE AND WHO ALL OF YOUR CUSTOMERS ARE!!! There is a time for that message. It comes when the customer is ready to know that information because they are ready to do business with you. Determine what points you want to make, and what you want the customer to walk away with? How will the customer view this meeting? Will they see it as a meeting that allowed them to gain knowledge or a favored outcome? When planning and outlining the message, determine what outcome you want from the meeting. Always plan for three outcomes:

1. What is the primary outcome that you want out of the meeting? You will tailor the meeting for this objective and will work to achieve it as your primary outcome. Maybe it is to get the customer to visit a site. Or to get the customer to support connecting you to the decision-maker. Perhaps it is to get the customer to schedule a deep dive in-person meeting with your technical team. In the commercial environment, it may be that you want the customer to sign on the dotted line.

2. If you fail to get the customer to agree to your first objective, you will need to have a planned second acceptable outcome.

In the above example, one goal was to get the customer to vi your site to see the solution at work. If they are hesita maybe a second favorable outcome might be to convince t customer to see a remote demonstration of your solution. white paper on the technology may be sufficient, presented your firm's technical expert. Get creative! The original goal to get your customer to observe your solution at work.

3. If you cannot achieve number two, have a third outcome pursuit. That may be to get the customer to agree to have the technical expert meet directly with your solution archite This encounter is but another version of your original objecti and desired outcome.

Of course, these are just examples. Your topic may entail no technical attributes. The point is always to have three (3) targ outcomes. Never leave a meeting empty-handed. If you do, y didn't plan the engagement appropriately. Let me repeat, <u>never lea the meeting without an outcome that keeps your foot in the door!</u>

Once you have the meeting planned, you will assign the task of getti the meeting scheduled, the date/timeframe for the meeting, a always have a comment section so that you can keep track of aspe in setting the meeting.

Details such as:

- the customer is on vacation until,
- placed call and waiting for return,
- scheduler is checking the customer's calendar,
- or the like.

Systematically track where you are in getting the meeting set up and what needs to change to make the next meeting a success.

Approach with the Right Message

To approach a potential customer with the right message, you need to know their hot buttons, and we have discussed how to do the research and understand those hot buttons. Once you have identified and thoroughly understand the customer's issue, it is time to revisit and refine your elevator speech - a statement designed to gain the customer's attention. Keep it short enough to message it on a quick elevator ride, maybe 30 seconds to one minute. Before exiting the elevator, present your business card and ask if you can meet to discuss further.

The customer is looking for help to address his/her immediate needs. When the business developer can recite the customer's dilemma and state how they can provide a solution, the customer will more likely

be interested in talking about it. Your elevator speech must have fo
crucial components:

- **Statement of the customer's need:** Mr. Jones, I understar
  that you are faced with the problem of quickly reducing tl
  time it takes to hire a new employee. You want to reduce tl
  time from 8 weeks to no more than 2 weeks as you are current
  losing valuable candidates to your competition.

- **How you solved the same problem for a customer
  comparable size, industry:** Mr. Jones, we solved that exa
  same problem for the ABC company just last year.

- **Provide quantifiable evidence:** With our solution they we
  able to reduce the time it took for them to hire from 2
  months to 1.5 weeks. Their recruiting numbers improved fro
  45% to 90% of targeted applicants.

- **Present your card and ask for a meeting to tell them how yc
  can work with them to achieve the same or similar succes**
  Here is my card. I would appreciate the opportunity to me
  with you to show you how we can help you solve your proble:
  with very similar success outcomes.

Most Business developers want to talk about their compan
successes, all of their customers, products, services, revenues, and a
about themselves. The customer does not want to talk about anythir
except what is of interest to him/her. They are not interested in yc

nor your company until they know that you and your company can address their specific needs.

When you do get the meeting, you will need to plan it so that you can approach properly, validate the needs, and present the right solution (answer) to the customer's problem. We will discuss the details of how to conduct the meeting later.

How to Get the Meeting with a Key Customer

There are several ways to get the meeting with the customer you have targeted for your marketing effort.

We have already discussed the use of the elevator speech. Your elevator speech can be used in any setting. It may be at a conference, it might also be in a grocery store, at a football game, in a restaurant, at the mall, in passing in the hallway – ANYWHERE! You will need several elevator speeches to be ready for any customer in your purview on any hot buttons that you have learned about in your research. In the previous chapter, we discussed research methods. Once you fully understand the customer's hot buttons and operational objectives, you can fully develop your elevator speech.

Another method used for getting a meeting is through a mutual acquaintance. It is essential to be on top of your game because you do

not want to embarrass the connector. They are laying their reputati
and relationship on the line to get you the meeting, and you mu
ensure that they come out of this encounter looking good. The be
way to thank the connector is to have your homework done a
conduct a great meeting.

Utilizing a consultant to set up the meeting is another option. The
consultants who work with the customer regularly and have gain
their trust and friendship can act as a connector to introduce you
the customer, provide a good reference and help get the meeting s
up.

One avenue that so many business developers overlook is t
administrative or executive assistant. My Executive Assistant not on
controlled my calendar, but in many cases, she would put people
my calendar and then explain to me why she thought it was vital f
me to meet with them. I noticed later that the business developers th
she did this for would do several things to get her attention. One, th
would stop in only to see her. If they were in the building, they wou
stop by to say, "Hi.' They might even bring her a bag of her favor
candy. During this stop in, they would not ask about me or try to g
on my schedule. They wanted to build a relationship with her. Th
would also eventually tell her how they could help me. She knew wh
I was working on, worried about, and what pressures were bei
placed on me by the Cabinet Secretary, Congress, the White Hous

etc. When she was convinced that this business developer could help relieve my stress, she would make sure that I met with them. They would also always thank her for scheduling the meetings and making sure that they got the time they needed with me. Never underestimate the power of the Executive Assistant.

If you have to resort to email or social media to try to get the meeting, be sure that you follow the steps you learned for the elevator speech: State the problem, how you have fixed it elsewhere, how you can help them. Give QUANTIFIABLE OUTCOMES that they will achieve working with you. Keep the email or request in social media short and to the point. Also, remember to *BUILD A RELATIONSHIP FIRST, if at all possible,* before asking for meetings and favors.

Be prepared with your elevator speech for a casual, informal meeting in a grocery store, on a golf course, a black tie, or any other setting.

Making a Positive First Impression

You now have "the" meeting! Let's talk about how to make a great first impression.

- Confirm the meeting before going. It would be best if you did this the day before the meeting. Sometimes the customer is dealing with critical issues, and they may need to move your session. If you show up and they were so involved that they did not have a chance to tell you that the timing isn't right, you may find yourself in the way, and that puts added pressure on your audience. Once you confirm the meeting, you can usually be assured that the customer will have time for you and has made your connection a priority.

- Arrive at least an hour early. You never know how long it will take to get through security. In some federal agencies, the building is so big that it may take a long time for the escort to get to you at the security station and take you to the meeting. Always keep in mind that the customer's time is precious, and you don't want to be the one who holds up their schedule. In fact, many customers will not attend the meeting if you are late. In addition to arriving at the security station 45 minutes early, you should arrive at the location at least 1 hour early because parking could be an issue. It is always better to arrive early and handle email or make phone calls instead of running the risk of being late. You also don't want to be disheveled when you arrive. Early arrival gives you time to settle in and be calm for the meeting.

- Have the contact information readily available for the security guard. In some agencies, for example, the U.S. Department of Agriculture, the security guards do not have the telephone numbers of the government employees with whom you are meeting.

- Make a great first impression
    - Dress appropriately for the meeting. I once had a customer discuss going to a meeting and whether they would wear khakis and no ties. I was blown away. When I asked them why they were even considering going in dressed so casually, they did not have an answer. They said they were weighing all options. THERE ARE NO OPTIONS! When meeting to conduct professional business, you must dress professionally. Many government personnel that you encounter will be wearing more casual attire, but I guarantee you that they expect you to be dressed professionally. There may be instances when you may meet with the lower-ranking personnel. Remember, an executive might also drop in on or be invited to the meeting. Most industries expect professional attire unless they tell you otherwise.

- Maintain good eye contact. This exudes confidence. If the customer senses that you are keen on the subject matter, they will view you as an expert and someone who can offer them the intelligence they are looking for.

- A firm handshake also helps convey confidence in yourself. The customer will pick up on that immediately. A weak

handshake reflects weakness and the sense that you are n
sure of yourself. Unfortunately, this may demote you in t
eyes of the customer, and you can lose a few points right o
of the chute.

- Plan how to execute the meeting. Develop your agenda a
  plan the dialogue. Always develop the encounter such th
  both you and the customer get the maximum benefit from t
  meeting. We will cover the anatomy of a successful meeti
  later.

  o Make sure you thank the executive assistant; this
    essential. We discussed the importance of a valu
    relationship with the assistant. Ensure that you stop
    his/her desk to say thank you. I remember seve
    individuals seeking to get on my calendar. They would s
    me at some event, and I would tell them that they cou
    meet with me. When they called my assistant, she wou
    not let them in even though they had been in the offi
    before. When I asked her why, she said, "I don't like the
    They are arrogant. They never speak to me. They lo
    beyond me. They never thanked me for the first meetin
    scheduled for them." For the others who treated her wi
    respect, she would make sure they got on the calendar.

- ○ Document the conversation and send an email thanking the customer for the meeting and providing a summary of the discussion and the to-do's or agreed-upon action plans and completion times and dates.

- Finally, NEVER LEAVE THE MEETING WITHOUT SCHEDULING A FOLLOW-UP MEETING.

Sales Approach – Conducting a Successful Customer meeting

You have been through all the preparation stages to ensure your readine for the engagement. You completed your research and now understar the customer's needs and hot buttons. You walked through the process building that trust relationship, and you have learned more about th customer's personality, likes, and dislikes. You understand the custome priorities and how the agency set those priorities. You know who th influencers are, and you know whom to go to for information. Yo scheduled and attended several meetings prior to and in preparation f the big meeting. You have gathered information from both internal ar external sources. You have reviewed the budget, and you know that th customer has justified the work which you are pursuing. You know whe the legislative branch of government stands on the solution you are sellir and what the appropriations committee has approved. You are aware any judicial branch issues that could throw a wrench into your plans. Yo know what the executive branch, including the White House/ Office Management and Budget as well as the Federal agency you are calling o have determined their priorities to be. Finally, you know the custome justification for your proposed solution. Now, the time has come! It time for the big meeting. You are on their calendar, and you are on yo way!

What do you do now?

THE FIRST RULE: CONFIRM YOUR MEETING.

The customer has a hectic schedule with many priorities, not of his/her own making. Sometimes, other priorities from the Cabinet Secretary, budget meetings, operations meetings, mission issues, or just issues, in general, will cause the customer's calendar to change. When I was a Chief Information Officer, I was more inclined to press on with the scheduled meeting and shift another priority if the Business Developer had confirmed with me ahead of time. If I had not received confirmation from the expected visitor, I might ask my secretary to reschedule them, especially if I have to handle something that I considered urgent. Please note that confirming does not guarantee that your meeting won't get rescheduled, which could happen while you are parking, but it is less likely. It is just common courtesy for any meeting to confirm before visiting.

THE SECOND RULE: ARRIVE EARLY.

Everyone has been in the lobby of a secured building and witnessed what it takes to get past security. It is a long, drawn-out process. I have been in the lobby of the Veterans Affairs headquarters building when a cleaning crew was going through security to enter the building. There were at least thirty (30) of them going through in a single file, and the guard desk operates on first-come-first-served. There is no cutting in the line just because you have a meeting. That process took

40 minutes to get all of them through. To my benefit, I had arriv
an hour early to the lobby. Otherwise, I could have missed my meeti:
if the cleaning crew had arrived a little later but ahead of me.

In addition to entry being a problem sometimes, parking could also
a significant problem. Regardless of what city you are in, parking
the street is rare downtown, and parking garages can fill up. You m
find yourself driving around the block searching. You may fi
yourself parking blocks away and dashing to your meeting plac
When a customer gives you 30 minutes for a meeting, and you arri
15 to 20 minutes late, it reflects poorly on you. Typically, the custom
has no choice but to cancel your meeting and is automatically left wi
a negative impression. To avoid delays from security, parking, traff
subway delays, flat tires, car accidents, road construction, and ma:
other challenges, always leave in time to arrive an hour early. If tl
meeting is critical to you, you will not mind getting there early. Y
can use the time waiting to go over your meeting plans and furth
prepare yourself during the wait.

THE THIRD RULE: SHAKE HANDS FIRMLY AND MAINTAIN EYE CONTACT.

When you meet the customer, your first handshake exchange
essential. If you perform a less than firm handshake, you will appe
timid, not trustworthy, and potentially perceived as weak. A fir

handshake signifies assuredness, confidence, mutual respect. Your handshake and body language must exude confidence and trust, and the handshake is a vital component of that "first impression."

Direct eye contact is also a sign of confidence and assuredness as well as respect. Look your customer directly in the eye! Regardless of the handshake, which can be practiced, by the way, I perceived a lack of trust, on several occasions, when a business development professional refused to look me in the eye. Without eye contact, and especially if the handshake was weak, I found myself viewing the individual as non-transparent, leaving me with little or no confidence in that person or their company. Once I had established that negative impression, I could not seriously consider their message. I understand that "eye contact" can also be practiced. But, human nature will, for the most part, reveal inconsistencies between verbal and non-verbal communication if you pay attention.

SIX STEPS OF A SUCCESSFUL CUSTOMER MEETING

It's showtime! You are ready to conduct that big meeting!
You will need to "carry" the meeting. <u>**YOU** are in charge of the flow and the outcome</u>. It is ultra-important that you plan this meeting from start to finish. If you go into the meeting unprepared, you will probably not get back in for a second meeting – or – you will find it extremely difficult to get that second meeting.

You want the customer to WANT you to come back! The key having a successful meeting is to follow the six steps that will ensu that the meeting flows correctly and provides a format for interchange of conversation between you and the customer. Elemer that can make your encounter with the customer <u>unsuccessful</u> are:

- Starting with a PowerPoint presentation
- Talking "at" the customer
- Giving the impression that you know everything
- Diving straight into a solution without vetting the needs wi the customer
- Not planning your desired outcome
- Not connecting with the customer

Follow the steps presented here to avoid these problems. You shou also memorize these steps and practice them over and over so that th become natural to you, and flow smoothly without detection from t. customer.

STEP ONE – Establish Rapport

It is essential to make the customer feel comfortable with you prior to getting into the meat of the meeting. People become more relaxed when they learn that they have something in  common with the person with whom they are meeting. It might be a sport, a hobby, family interests, friends in common, and many other things. It is ideal when the customer opens up about something important to them before getting into the business portion of the conversation. It would help if you learned something personal about the person you are meeting with before the meeting. Did they receive an award? Did a family member just get married? Maybe there is a new baby in the family. Do you both play the same sport? Perhaps you both belong to the same organization. You can learn these things by talking to people who know them, reading about them, or observing something in their office. If you see a picture of a football team, you may ask about that. If you see an award, you may want to ask about it and congratulate them. Maybe you see a little putt-putt toy prompting you to ask about golf. Perhaps there is a college banner in their office, which you can discuss. There are so many things that you can learn or see about the customer that can spark a personal conversation. Establishing rapport should only take 2-3 minutes because you need most of your time to discuss the subject of the meeting. But that 2-3 minutes are critical to getting the meeting off to a pleasant start. Take it seriously. And remember, it is not about you; it's about the customer and giving them a chance to talk about things going on in their lives. By the way, if they mention a need, like looking for a golf course, or wanting to join an organization that you belong to, this is the time to offer a favor. You now have an alternative means to establish a relationship.

KEEP IT POSITIVE – DO NOT DISCUSS POLITICS OR RELIGION

STEP TWO - Gain interest

If the customer is going to spend 30 minutes or more talking to you, it is crucial to give them a good reason to want to spend the time. The easiest way to do this is to use that "elevator speech" we spoke about previously. The elevator speech is an attention-getter, and maybe what you used to get the meeting.

It has four components:

1. statement of a problem that they are having as you have learned,

2. how you solved this problem at an entity similar in size and complexity as the organization with whom you are meeting,

3. quantifiable benefits obtained by the client for whom you solved the problem,

4. ask them if they are interested in hearing how you can help them achieve the same or similar quantifiable benefits.

STEP THREE – Understand customer needs

Step three is the most critical, and the one most often skipped. The inexperienced business developer is anxious to rush into their comfort zone.  They start explaining their product or service. They never take the time to explore with the customer what indeed are their needs. This faux pas will cause the customer to want to end the meeting quickly, and the business development pro may never get another

chance to meet. The customer has specific requirements and p:
points that they are dealing with daily. It is these requireme
that are the priority and are the focus for resolution. When y
come in not focusing on their needs, but instead focusing on y
solution, which may not have anything to do with what they ne
it becomes a complete waste of the customer's time. You must
careful not to ask what the needs are. Asking about the objecti
and pain points indicates to the customer that you did not do y
homework. The customer has no desire to do your homework
you. The most effective approach is to state what you believe
the needs and then ask for validation. Most times, the custor
will expand on what you have already learned. This approach
the customer know that you did your homework, and they
more willing now to give more detailed information.
customer will likely provide more details about additi
problems that you may not be able to obtain elsewhere.

To begin this portion of the meeting, you state each probler
challenge that you have researched. It would be best if you di
try to cover everything you know because you will run out of t
Now is the time to get the customer's input and allow them to
to you about their quandaries. Listen carefully and ask rele
questions. An example of how to walk through this step follo

Mr. Customer, I heard you speak at the association breakfast about your need to reduce processing time for hiring candidates. You stated that it currently takes four months, and you need to get that to no more than two weeks. I imagine that you are losing key candidates with the long processing times you are experiencing. Can you tell me more about this challenge and the obstacles you face? Allow the customer to respond. Listen carefully and ask questions as the conversation develops. REMEMBER, this is the time to get as much from the customer as you can. Learn to listen and listen to learn. Write down what the customer is saying and be prepared to repeat his/her own words back.

If you have learned details about their timeframe or the spending constraints, ask about those and show that you have done that research and write down the answers. These written answers will become very important when you are presenting your solution in STEP FOUR. At the end of this "discussion," (not presentation), you will repeat what you have learned back to the customer to ensure that you got it right and that the customer concurs with your understanding of the  needs. Complete the puzzle with the knowledge you gain from this very productive discussion.

STEP FOUR - Present the solution

Step Four is the step that mo BDers and their architects a anxiously awaiting. Th opportunity to present the solutio is where they believe they ca impress the customer – shine! Th step, however, can be yo downfall if you do not execute th

previous steps correctly. Note, this is the first point in the custom encounter where it MAY be appropriate to use a PowerPoi presentation. However, this is your very first meeting with th customer, and there may still be follow-on meetings and mo discussion to get to the point where the customer is ready to g into solution details. REMEMBER, reserve PowerPoi presentations for SOLUTION DETAILS!

Now you want to present your solution based upon the discussio of the needs you have had with the customer. It is essential durir this time to use the customer's own words that you gained in th "needs" discussion to justify your solution. Present the feature advantages, and benefits of your solution point by point. For eac discussion point, repeat what the customer has said to yc concerning a particular need and how your solution solves th concern and benefits the customer. Be very careful during this step not to get caught up in all of your knowledge that you take over the conversation. Never talk "at" the customer, but instead dialogue with them. To reinforce dialogue, ask for their opinion on what you have just presented.

For example, "Mr. Customer, you stated that an automated search of the applicant's qualifications would save at least 4-6 weeks off your current manual process. Do you see how our innovation will benefit your current process? Although results may vary, how much time do YOU think our feature would save your team?"

Be quiet and let the customer answer!

The customer may respond, "Wow! This capability would be an incredible addition to our method and could further speed the process by weeks. I see this innovation alone shaving at least four weeks off manually searching through candidate applications!".

At the end of this interactive exchange of needs, features, benefits, and customer reactions, summarize the solution using the customer's own words and comments. Sometimes it makes sense to take someone to the meeting with you to take notes and be ready to repeat the customer's feedback. While the customer is responding, be sure to capture all vital points the customer is

making in mapping their need to your solution so you c
summarize the conversation, using their same comments.
essence, the customer is now beginning to sell your solutior
strategy to him/herself!

STEP FIVE – Handle Objections

You have now successfully
established a positive connection
with the customer. You have
also given the customer a reason
to want to spend these 30
minutes to an hour with you.
You explored the real needs and
priorities of the customer and learned so much more from t
customer's point of view. You presented to the customer how y
can help them solve the problem. You're feeling pretty good ar
think it is a 'slam dunk"!

You are now at the time to ask for one of your desired outcom
and suddenly the customer throws up an objection. For exampl
you ask the customer to visit your customer briefing center to s
the solution in action or possibly a visit to your customer site whe
your product or service is proven successful. You are a litt
surprised when the customer comes back with a response such a

"Well, I don't think we have the skills and talent to implement your solution!" How you handle this objection will determine success or failure.

To handle an objection there are several things you need to do seamlessly:

- Listen intently to what the customer is saying about what their concerns are. Don't become defensive. Just allow the customer to explain his/her hesitation to proceed.
- Repeat the customer's concern to make sure you fully understand. Don't just start telling them why they are wrong. Repeat the concern back to the customer and ask if you comprehend it correctly.
- Show empathy to the customer and answer the objection stating that you understand their concerns. You might say something along the lines of, "I recognize why you might think that implementing such a comprehensive solution would require skills that you feel don't currently exist in your organization. The customer that I'd like you to observe felt the very same way. They will attest that the industry acumen, support talent, and project plans brought to the table by my team guided their current staff through a successful implementation. Their team quickly gained the skills as we guided them through the entire process.

They built such tremendous skills with my teams' guidan
that we were able to transition operations over to tl
customer ahead of schedule. Today, they are runnii
successfully on their own. A visit will prove to be i
incredible benefit, allowing you to ask them about how tl
worked for them." Gauge the customer's reaction to yo
response.

- Ask if you have addressed their concern.
- If not, ask for clarification and try again.

STEP SIX – Close

Once you have addressed all
objections, it is time for "The
Close." You know what you want
from the meeting, and you have
planned for three outcomes in case
you don't get the first or even the
second. ASK FOR THE
OUTCOME YOU PLANNED FOR AND BE QUIET! W;
for the customer to respond.

I have witnessed too many BDers ask for the close and kee
talking. They soon talk themselves right out of the outcome th

wanted. When the customer says "yes," confirm the outcome and close the meeting. *Babbling on can only get you in trouble.*

TEMPLATE FOR CUSTOMER MEETING PLANNING

The following template can help you plan your customer meeting. Always take plenty of time to plan this critical meeting. Nothing else is more important in building that Trusted Partnership with the customer.

Step 1: Establish Rapport – Find a topic to discuss to relax the customer and make a connection. You may be able to find something to discuss from a friend, employee, something in the office of the customer, other

Example: Thank you for taking the time to meet with us today. I see you have pictures of motorcycles in your office. How long have you been a Harley Davidson fan?

Write:

Step 2: Create Interest – Capture the customer's attention to hear you out. Get them interested in what you plan to accomplish in the meeting. Must be something in it for them

Example: I understand that you are challenged with the complexity of software renewals, the cost of software in your enterprise, and software

---

maintenance costs. My customer at the ABC agency was faced with the same problem. We were able to provide them with a solution which we implemented in 3 months showing results in 1 week. They reduced their software maintenance spend by 37%, reduced software audit costs by 80%, and reclaimed annual savings of $466K out of $1.7M spent. I am here to show you how we can help you achieve the same or better results and solve your software problems?

Write:

Step 3: Understand Needs – A discussion with the customer to make sure that you completely understand the needs before trying to present a solution Tell the customer what you understand about his needs from the research you've done. Ask for validation and take copious notes. Summarize by reciting back to the customer what he/she has stated about the needs.

Example: Mr. Customer, one of your needs as I have researched it, is that you want to reduce the cost of software renewals. You are currently spending $1.7 M and you want to reduce that amount by $450,000. Do I understand that correctly? (Let customer respond). Are there any resource constraints that might prohibit you from meeting this goal? Can you elaborate? (Let customer respond). How are you currently planning to attack this issue? (Let customer respond. Take notes on what customer is saying.

Move to next need. Same as above until needs are discussed.

Write:

Step 4: Present the Solution – Discuss with the customer how you can bring solution/solutions to address his/her needs. Address each need with a solution. Use customers words when speaking of the needs. Describe the function, advantage, and benefit of your solution for each need. Ask the customer how he/she sees this solution addressing the need. Write their words. Do not use super technical terms. Speak to mission.

Example: Mr. Customer, you stated that you want to reduce the software renewal cost by 25% or more. You stated that the modern software is complex and consists (typically) of thousands of files per product. It is very difficult for software managers to ensure that such software is authorized and needed. Also, I understood you to say that 50% of your software is over-subscribed on unused software assets. Correct?

What we can do is help you implement a Software Waste Management solution which will a. Provide a single interface into your normalized software inventory, b. Provide you with deep insight into application usage and c. Provide you with an automated and scalable methodology to remove software which is not being utilized by end-users. As a result, you will be able to more accurately know what software needs to be renewed and at what levels. (Expand) How do you see this part of the solution benefiting you as you work to reduce cost?

You also stated that you want to reduce cost of maintenance.........
(continue with other discussed needs and solutions)

At the end, Summarize each need and corresponding solution. Ask
customer for agreement.
Write:

Step 5: Handle Objection – If customer throws out an objection, such as
he/she is not sure that they can afford such a solution, empathize with them
stating that you understand how they might feel that way, explain further
why they should not be concerned and ask if you answered their concern,
and go for the close again. If you see that they are not ready to have their
direct reports attend a demonstration yet, move to your second choice of an
outcome. Ask them, for example, if they'd like a white paper explaining in
detail how the solution would work on their specific needs. Continue this
process until they agree to your outcome and you have another audience with
them or the right people in the account.
Write:

Step 6: Close – Ask for the outcome you came prepared to gain from the
meeting. You should have come with 3 possible outcomes in priority order.

Example: So, Mr. Customer, we have looked at your needs and I have
explained several solutions that address your needs. You agreed that these

solutions will provide you with the software management and cost reductions you are looking to achieve. You described how the solutions we discussed will solve your problems. What I'd like to do is schedule a meeting to come back and demonstrate this solution to you and your team. Can we get with your administrative assistant now to get that meeting on your calendar?

Write

WHAT TO DO AFTER THE MEETING

Once the meeting has ended, ask the customer to walk with you to his/her administrator's desk to get the meeting scheduled. Thank the admin for setting the meeting and be sure the admin knows how to reach you.

Give them your business card and write "Thank you" on the card! This exchange will help them remember who you are. Once you are back to your office, send a "thank you" note with a summary of the meeting and the agreed-upon action items. Copy the admin and thank him/her as well. Back at the office, get the meeting on everyone's calendar, get the scheduled visit set up right away so that you have time to handle any problems that might arise. Do not wait until the last minute to schedule the customer visit (in this example)!

DO'S AND DON'TS IN THE CUSTOMER MEETING

There are a few essential things to know and follow when meeti
with the customer:

1. Do NOT bring a PowerPoint presentation to the first meetin
   And maybe not to subsequent sessions until the time
   appropriate. The proper time for a PowerPoint is when t
   customer is ready to understand the details of your solution.

2. Be a good listener. A meeting with a customer is a time to let t
   customer talk and validate the objectives and pain points y
   uncovered with your research. The purpose of these encounte
   with a customer is to understand their particular problem as mu
   as possible. You want to develop the very best solution to addre
   their distinct dilemma. So, listen carefully and never monopoli
   the conversation.

3. Give ample time for the meeting. Get there early. Make sure th
   you park where you do not have to rush out to your car to "fe
   the meter" during the meeting. Sometimes a customer may
   ready to see you early, and that may add to the time they ha
   allocated for you. Plan to arrive an hour early as we have discuss
   earlier. It is unacceptable to be late for a customer meeting f
   ANY reason!

4. Make no assumptions. Your assumptions could be very wrong and if you rely on them, it may take the conversation down the wrong path. Clear up any theories or questions you have made right up front with the customer so that you can have successful results.

5. Don't name drop. It is appropriate to talk about people you mutually know. When you start telling the customer about all the "important" people you know, the customer will view you as pompous. In my career, I have experienced business development professionals tell me how well they knew my Cabinet Secretary, how well they knew my Congressman, how well they knew people in the White House. What a waste of valuable meeting time. I remember thinking, "Well, why don't you go talk to them! It's obvious that you don't need me!" Name dropping, to this day, still grates on my nerves!

Conclusion

In this book, I have taken you through the systematic approach becoming a great business developer. It is a step-by-step process tha when understood, practiced regularly, and mastered, will push you to t "head of the pack"!

I am uniquely qualified to provide this instruction because I have had t privilege of sitting on both sides of that desk. I was a very successf salesperson with one of the top companies in the industry, eventua teaching sales to their executives. As a senior executive in the company was regularly called by business developers at all levels, where I mentor them to success.

As a government "C level", I saw the dos and don'ts for many years. I ha gained the inside experience of government business and know what takes to succeed in that marketplace. I have talked to many of r colleagues. They, too, listen to business developers regularly and ha shared their disappointments with the lack of knowledge, never doi their homework, and naive approaches to doing business with the fede government. They have told me how they had ended meetings becau they could not take it anymore. They have also told me what made the want to continue building a win-win relationship with those who call on them correctly. They have expressed to me the same feelings tha experienced with many business developers myself as an executive in the federal government.

As stated in the introduction I explained that there are 8 phases to becoming a trusted partner with your customer. We have touched on, and you have learned all of those phases in this book. We offer classes in Parker Group Consulting that take you for a much deeper dive into these teachings. We also provide workshops and templates so that you can practice and become so familiar with the process that it becomes second nature to you. Our readers and students who follow this systematic approach to business development become the "very best" in the industry. They can do it in their sleep.

Along with Business Development, the professional should understand Capture and Operations Management processes that lead to winning recompetes and growing business in the account. In our series of course offerings and other books, we teach these practice areas of the framework to mature your Business Development Life Cycle expertise.

Take this book your reference guide. Highlight those areas that you rely on the most and practice, practice, practice. Reach out to us for more in-depth knowledge by enrolling in our training courses for the deep dive sessions with workshops, role playing, and template use.

I want to take this opportunity to thank Mike Rice, who added some of the capture strategies from his book and insight into today's federal government procurement practices. It was great collaborating with him. His book, which he shared with me, called "In Pursuit – Business Development Life Cycle", teaches Capture processes that are well-practiced by businesses pursuing government contract opportunities.

I hope you enjoyed the lessons learned here and will practice them to become the absolute best at what you do, and we look forward to seeing you in our classes.

Visit us at www.parkergroupconsulting.com

Made in the USA
Middletown, DE
17 November 2020

24303724R00071